FIJI

A LOVE STORY

Ajay Singh (1950–2020) was educated at Modern School and St. Stephen's College at Delhi and Canterbury University in New Zealand. He started his career in journalism with the *Fiji Times* and had a brief stint with *Surya India, India Today* and *Morning Echo*, a tabloid of the Hindustan Times Group in Delhi. He joined the All India Kisan Trust as its Managing Trustee in 1980 with Chaudhary Charan Singh as its Chairman. He entered politics in 1986 as Member of the Legislative Council in UP. He was elected Member of Parliament from Agra in 1989 and was Union Deputy Minister for Railways in the V P Singh-led Government. Subsequently, he headed several cultural and educational organisations as the chairman of their governing bodies. He served as India's High Commissioner to Fiji Islands during 2005-07. Later he remained engaged in the community and social work and 2013 onwards was President of the All India Sarv Jat Mahasabha.

FIJI
A LOVE STORY
Memoirs of an Unconventional Diplomat

AJAY SINGH

SHIPRA

₹ 550
US$ 22
ISBN: 978-93-91978-35-8

2023 Impression
(First Published in India in 2022)

Fiji: A Love Story
Memoirs of an Unconventional Diplomat

Published by:
SHIPRA PUBLICATIONS
LG 18-19, Pankaj Central Market
I.P. Ext., Patparganj, Delhi 110092, India
Tel.: +91 11 2223 5152; 96500 28065
E-mail: info@shiprapublication.com
www.shiprapublication.com

Dedicated to My Muse Shiromani Tiwari Singh

Tum jo hamare meet na hote
Geet ye mere geet na hote
Hans ke jo tum ye rang na bharte
*Khwab ye mere khwab na hote**

(Had you not been my love,
These songs would not had been of my songs.
Had you not coloured them with smile,
These dreams of mine, would had never been there.)

(*A song from film 'Aashiq', 1962, Lyricist - Shailendra)

"And why does it make you sad to see how everything hangs by such thin and whimsical threads? Because you are a dreamer, an incredible dreamer, with the tiny spark hidden somewhere inside you which cannot die, which even you cannot kill or quench and which tortures you horribly because all the odds are against its continually burning. In the midst of the foulest decay and putrid savagery, this spark speaks to you of beauty, of human kindness and warmth, goodness, of greatness, of heroism and martyrdom and speaks to you of love."

Soul on Ice
Eldridge Cleaver

Contents

Foreword

RT HON SIR ANAND SATYANAND
PO BOX 9062 MARION SQUARE
WELLINGTON 6141 NEW ZEALAND
TEL: +64 21 586 409
EMAIL: anand.satyanand@gmail.com

India and Fiji and New Zealand provide a huge contrast, one, the most populous and culturally diverse nation on earth, one a group of Pacific Islands where Indian people have made a substantial contribution, and the last, also a small country with an even smaller Indian component in its make-up. Despite being half way around the world from each other, there are a number of things which the countries share - use of the English language, a history in times past of being colonies of Britain, parliamentary, legal and banking systems of similar kinds, a tradition of a vigorous Press, membership of the Commonwealth and lastly a commitment to democracy which has mostly endured.

It is not usual for any person to make their mark in more than one country. However, in the case of the author of this book, there is a graphic example of one who has done just this. Ajay Singh was born, raised and educated in India and spent most of his working life in that country. He studied there as a young man, then came Fiji and on to New Zealand for post graduate study and qualification. He lived and worked for a short time in New Zealand and then for more substantial periods in Fiji before returning to India.

The linkage between Fiji and India is a case of repetition because his grandfather and his father before him had had this in lives to do with indentured labour and government service, and had worked in both countries. Ajay himself, after training as a journalist in New Zealand, and working here, worked in that profession in Fiji and then in India. Notably, he married in Fiji and he and his wife Siromani Maharaj, kept up their connections everywhere they had been. Being gregarious and optimistic about the world around him, led Ajay Singh to a stint in Indian Federal politics, inclusive of holding office as a Minister. After that became spent, he returned to his fundamental career of journalism combining that with an abiding interest in public and international affairs. It was no surprise to those who knew him, that he received a brief to become India's High Commissioner to Fiji which he undertook at a very difficult time in that country when commitment to democracy was sorely tested.

The tapestry of his life is therefore an interesting one to relate. There is also a remarkable comparison to be made, of which the reader learns, that Ajay's father, Bhagwan Singh, had himself been a successful Indian High Commissioner to Fiji, more than thirty years before his son. It was from there that the young Ajay came to New Zealand to further his education.

Ajay devoted his time in recent years to an account of his activities and likewise an array of insights and opinions which will challenge and amuse the reader.

I am proud of being regarded by him as a friend and confirm the relationship of which he speaks in the book about the link between ourselves, our parents and grandparents. I was thus delighted to receive a request from the author Professor Mahavir Singh to write a foreword on the basis that it was apparently Ajay's wish that this be so. Ours was an individual friendship going back to student days and on his regular visits to New Zealand he would make the time to connect with many of his friends, including myself and family. Ajay was a legendary conversationalist with a prodigious memory, and an ability to register opinions without fear. Each of those traits - warmth towards friends, recall of detail, and telling the story inimitably, make this book a fine and warm-hearted piece of work.

One of the better things about the book is the challenge it presents to the readers of today and especially the young, that the world and its interests know no bounds and that people whose background may be humble have potential to make a telling contribution far beyond their place of birth and financial circumstance.

Anand Satyanand
Wellington New Zealand July 2021

The author of this foreword is the Rt Hon' Sir Anand Satyanand GNZM, QSO, PBSA 19th Governor-General of New Zealand, (20062011) awardee of the Pravasi Bharatiya Samman Award in 2011 from Smt Pratibha Patil, President of India

Prologue

Mahavir Singh*

The author of this autobiography started writing his memoirs and sadly left it incomplete when he passed away in mid 2020 prematurely but undoubtedly to keep a tryst with his departed love. He procrastinated long in deciding which story from his life was the best to share. His life was enriched by vivid experiences and lasting relationships formed during varied careers over a life spanning some seven decades. He was trained as a journalist, groomed as a community leader, dragged into the uncertainties of politics including a short span as a Union Minister and followed his father's footsteps as a diplomat.

One could say his life was destined by fate when his great grandfather Ram Chandar, left Agra for Fiji, recruited as an indentured labourer. His fate was sealed when he married his life's love, Shiromani, in Fiji where his father Bhagwan Singh, the grandson of a "girmitiyas" (as the indentured labour were referred to in Fiji), became the first Indian High Commissioner after the colony became independent.

His last active assignment was as the Indian High Commissioner to Fiji Islands. After aborting other themes, he finally decided that *the* book he would write would be on the saga of his family and Fiji. The lockdown period from the end of March 2020 forced him to concentrate on writing as all his outdoor activities and tours came to a halt. He finished three chapters in April and sent them to friends for their comments. The feedback he received was highly encouraging. His story was gripping and his style was much appreciated, steeling his determination to finish the book at the earliest.

I got to know Ajay Singh well over the years. When he was High Commissioner in Fiji, I served as his cultural counsellor in the High Commission and as Director of the Indian Cultural Centre. Thus, I accompanied him to different parts of Fiji Islands on his many official

---

* Former Director, ICC and Cultural Counsellor High Commission of India in Fiji Islands. He has also been Director, MAKAIAS & EZCC at Kolkata, Professor of History at Pondicherry University, Hon. Fellow at the University College London and Professor & Dean Academics at GBU, Gr. Noida.

and social visits and have first hand information of so many events and happenings of his tenure in Fiji.

He had a passion for poetry and literature and books were his obsession. He had a very rich and eclectic collection of more than 4,000 books in his study, including early encyclopaedias, travel books, religious commentaries and tomes on history, politics, international affairs, biographies, social commentary and the arts. A whole section was devoted to writings about Fiji.

He not only collected books but was an avid reader and knew each book in his collection intimately. He knew exactly where to find almost any volume one asked for. He would take great pleasure in producing a volume on whatever topic was being discussed during the evening pre-dinner drinks in his study.

As a bibliophile, he continued to collect books until his final days. Om Book Shop in Gurgaon and Bahrisons in Khan market were his most frequented haunts. Once he was engrossed in browsing at Bahrisons with a Pablo Neruda volume tucked under one arm when he heard a voice from behind, "*Jaat log kabse Pablo Neruda padhne lage*". He looked back and found Vasundhara Raje, another bookworm politician, grinning. The Jats have a great sense of humour and capacity to laugh at themselves.

Urdu *shairi* was his passion and his modest knowledge of Urdu was no deterrent. Works by Mirza Ghalib, Mir Taqi Mir, Mohammad Iqbal, Ibrahim Zouq and Nazir Akbarabadi graced his study. Urdu poetry has *nazms, shers* and couplets befitting every occasion. Ajay Singh emboldened by a few drinks would recite these tellingly at social occasions. His memory for them was astounding but his use of them as appropriate commentary was captivating.

Ajay Singh noted some of the oft repeated and quoted shers in his pocket diary and had learnt them by heart for recitation at the appropriate time. When in a philosophical mood, he would recite Nazir's Banjaranama, "*Sab thaat pada reh jayega jab laad chalega banjara*" or quote Faiz Ahmad Faiz, *"Lambi hai gham ki shaam, magar shaam hi to hai"* to show a ray of hope for some gloomy, unhappy face. He had more than a dozen quotes ready in his memory.

He received many invitations for all kinds of events ranging from seminars, book launches, old boys get-togethers, and political meetings in Delhi and outside the capital. He tried to attend as many as he could but one event he never liked to miss was a book launch. He would attend even if he was able to attend it for a while. His objective: to come back with a copy of the book signed by the author.

I remember the launch of Lt. General Zameeruddin Shah's book *The Sarkari Mussalman* at the India International Centre. His son Omar sent the invitation through my son Navneet (they had studied together at St Xavier's, Kolkata). Knowing Ajay Singh's avid interest in books he insisted that we both must attend the book launch. By the time we reached IIC, the auditorium was full and there was no space to even stand. Zameer's brother, the film star Naseeruddin Shah, and popular film actor Gul Panag and a couple of other Bollywood luminaries besides the usual high profile crowd of Delhi was present. Seeing that there was no chance to get in we bought two books from the stall outside and were about to leave when we spotted Gen Shah coming back from the washroom. Ajay hastened to interrupt him and asked, "General Shah would you mind autographing a copy of your book?" The general was visibly in a hurry, but he made Ajay's day when he smiled and obliged and rushed to the auditorium.

He was generous with his books. When ordering books online would often order multiple copies: one for his study and the rest for presenting to people. During his air travels, if he had a bit of extra time available before boarding the plane, the only place he visited was a book shop. During his foreign travels he carried several books. He would read them and on returning would give them to friends.

Prof. Biman Prasad, former Dean of the University of South Pacific and now Member of Parliament and deputy leader of opposition in Fiji Parliament, recalled to me how Ajay Singh had presented him with Gurcharan Das' *Difficulty of Being Good* when Prof. Prasad had invited Ajay to deliver a lecture at his university in 2011. Prof. Prasad cherishes the book even today, finding it relevant in his profile as a public person, because the book's main theme is an elaboration on the meaning of Dharma through the characters of Mahabharata.

Rarely would Ajay go to sleep without reading a book for at least an hour. The last book he was reading before going to hospital from where he never returned home in June 2020, was *The Last Sunset: The Rise & the Fall of the Lahore Durbar* by Capt. Amarinder Singh. The book was found in his bedroom with the bookmark on page 120.

After Shiromani's death in November 2017, he was inconsolable and very lonely. I would often get summoned to visit him mainly to keep him company and help him in organising his private archives and personal papers. We spent hours in his study reminiscing and talking.

Ajay was a long time sufferer of rheumatoid arthritis which affected most of his joints. The pain was often insufferable yet he maintained a cheerful demeanour for those around him. He found it hard to sleep and spent many a night reading and listening to his favourite songs which he selected for their nostalgic romance. He was missing his love. When he would eventually come down to his study around midmorning, he would recount his night's mental adventures. The chapters of his autobiography which were in their final draft were often discussed.

A new stage was set for India-Fiji relations when Prime Minister Narendra Modi paid an official visit to Fiji Islands on November 19, 2014. It was after 33 years that an Indian Prime Minister had visited Fiji, the previous, and the only other visit by a Prime Minister being by Indira Gandhi in 1981.

P M Modi's visit to Fiji opened up new avenues, taking the India-Fiji relationship to new heights. The restoration of democracy in Fiji, the adoption of a new constitution in September 2013 and a resounding victory for Prime Minister Voreqe Bainimarama in the first elections held in September 2014 after he captured power in a military coup in 2006, had paved the way for stronger bilateral ties. Prime Minister Modi addressed the Fiji Parliament, the first foreign dignitary to do so after Fiji's return to democracy. He was also shown the carved wooden high chair of the speaker presented by India to Mr. R D Patel, the first Speaker elected after the first elections in post-independent Fiji, which was still being used by the speaker of Fiji.

Ajay was the strongest votary of widening India's ties with Fiji Islands and the larger South Pacific region. Many of the Pacific Island nations are mere specks on the world map but straddle enormous swathes of territorial waters with large Exclusive Economic Zones. He was consulted by the Ministry of External Affairs when Prime Minister Modi's three-nation tour to Myanmar, Australia and Fiji was being planned. He spoke to senior Ministry officials and briefed them on India's historic ties with Fiji. He also explained the connections with the other Pacific Islands and the need to keep engaged with them. India has had warm ties with Tonga, Nauru and Papua New Guinea. He stressed the significance of small development assistance programmes and how India can offer small and medium projects that affect the lives of the tiny island communities

Modi was welcomed in Fiji with traditional rituals. In Suva he had a meeting with the leaders and representatives of a dozen Island nations belonging to the Pacific Islands Forum. Aside from credit lines and developmental assistance, he made an offer to the Pacific leaders to develop a Pan Pacific Island project for tele-medicine and tele-education, similar to the one developed for African Union states. It was a very successful tour that was followed by an India-Pacific Island summit in India the next year. In turn, Fiji provided assistance to India's Mangalyaan Mission to Mars, extending logistic support through their infrastructure and base in Fiji for tracking the satellite.

Ajay Singh was working on some writings on these recent developments and had had discussions with Prof. Ganesh Chand, Vice-Chancellor of Fiji National University, who had hosted a public meeting for Prime Minister Modi. He even thought seriously about making a documentary or a full fledged film on his great grandmother Padam Kaur alias Porbotti and her heroic struggle as a "girmitiya" woman which had gone on to shape the life of future generations of her family.

Ajay for me was like an elder brother, a mentor and friend. I became his confidante at a time when he needed protection and support the most. He would describe me to his friends as an "abiding companion" in his most critical days. Shiromani was very concerned about his drinking and smoking as she was certain that both compromised his health and well being. She would often be very stern in her admonitions.

I on the other hand, although concerned, thought that he performed better and was more spirited when he was relaxed. His addictions were life long and started when he was at high school. However, Ajay Singh was always able to maintain his dignity, be courteous and spell binding as a raconteur in whichever circle he was performing, be it with politicians, old school friends or his literary comrades. Ajay liked people and was very considerate and compassionate. He and Shiro had a magnificent home, beautifully furnished with thematic decorations that bore witness to their love of art and culture. However, each article carried with it some special memory shared by the couple.

Ajay Singh was born into privilege. His father held important posts in Government and as such he had access to the best school and college in Delhi and he was socially well connected.

Ajay was an enigma. He was privileged yet strongly connected to the working class and villagers. His political activism matured when the politics of non-Congressism was heating up. His connections were wide and he worked with prominent politicians of this time. He was young when he became a junior Union Minister. Some have said he was too honest to have been a successful politician. He himself would laughingly reflect on his short but colourful times when he was successful in elections.

His political training began with Chaudhary Charan Singh, former Prime Minister and a stalwart of Indian politics. Chaudhary Charan Singh established the All India Kisan Trust with himself as its President and appointed young Ajay Singh as the Managing Trustee. Working with Chaudhary Sahib was a great learning for Ajay Singh and shaped his worldview. But he regarded George Fernandez as his mentor and as a major influence in the evolution of his political philosophy. Interestingly a prominent picture in his study shows him with George and others with the Dalai Lama.

Ajay was an avowed atheist yet he kept a picture of Sathya Sai Baba in his drawer! He performed a Govardhan parikrama to appease his devout mother and even offered a *chadar* on the *mazar* of Khwaja Moinuddin Chisti's Dargah at Ajmer on the advice of his friends who believed that when medicines don't help, *duayen* (prayers) sometimes do. This was when Shiromani was combating cancer. He did it all.

The war clubs in the entrance lobby of Ajay and Shinro's house were a valued farewell present to them from the Fijian military barracks. Whilst Ajay did not approve of "coups d'etat" he did recognise that with time one should move on with living and engage with people so that the future could be more harmonious. Thus one of his most significant contributions to international diplomacy was to convince the Indian government to allow Fiji back into the Commonwealth of Nations.

Alas time waits for none and it certainly did not wait for Ajay Singh to complete his long awaited autobiography. What we offer now are some chapters which were written by Ajay whilst others are of a biographical nature added by compiling his notes from his laptop and personal papers for completeness. No liberty has been taken with the views expressed by him. The pictures have also been chosen by me but many of them occupied positions of prominent exposure in Ajay's study so I am sure he would approve their inclusion.

This book was made possible only with invaluable assistance and inputs from Ajay Singh's sister Shubha Singh, an acclaimed writer on Fiji and Indian diaspora affairs, and Dr. Rajat Gyaneshwar, a close family friend of Ajay, and a reputed gynaecologist and obstetrician who divides his time between Australia and Fiji. During his last two visits to India I had witnessed Dr. Gyaneshwar spending long evenings with Ajay Singh in his study discussing girmit history, developments in Fiji and analysing in hindsight the days of Ajay Singh as Indian High Commissioner and his dealings with the two regimes under Laisenia Qarase and Frank Bainimarama.

I owe a debt of gratitude to Mr. Ajay Kumar, a retired senior journalist and a friend of Ajay Singh from college, who did several rounds of reading of the book's draft, raised many queries and sought many clarifications on key points. His editing has helped make the storyline understandable to a lay reader. My interaction with him was a great learning experience.

My very first meeting with him during a visit to Goa in January 2020 was memorable. A fellow politician friend of Ajay Singh, Mr. Kamal Morarka, an industrialist, philanthropist and a self-proclaimed "left of the Centre" politician, had generously offered his seaside resort *Casa Bela* to stay in Goa. One evening we forsook the pleasures of the beach resort to travel half an hour to a beautiful bungalow in a hill station-like setting.

The bungalow had a spacious verandah with a nice view. The house itself was tastefully decorated with a small swimming pool inside the courtyard. Ajay Singh introduced me to the bungalow's dwellers, Ajay Kumar and his wife, Gouri Salvi. While having coffee in the verandah both Ajays were talking about some manuscript and I remember Ajay Kumar saying, "You send me the text as soon as it is ready and leave the rest to me." I did not grasp at that time that they were discussing this book.

To Rt. Hon'ble Sir Anand Satyanand, former Governor-General of New Zealand and recipient of the Pravasi Bharatiya Samman Award from India, who has strong family connections of three generations with the family of Ajay Singh, I owe special thanks for the book's foreword.

My first and the late Ajay Singh's last meeting with Sir Anand was in January 2019 in Wellington. Mr. Graeme Waters, a former New Zealand High Commissioner to India, and Mrs. Audrey Waters, an alumni of Jamia Millia Islamia University in Delhi, hosted a dinner in honour of Mr. Ajay Singh in a Wellington restaurant and invited some common friends including "Sir Anand and Lady Susan Satyanand". It was my first face to face with Sir Anand whose name was familiar to me for a long time.

Ajay Singh and I were accompanied from Auckland to Wellington by another three -generation old family friend, Tony Bidesi. In Wellington Ajay Singh, Tony and I attended the wedding of the daughter of his Canterbury days friend Anna Cottrell who he treated as his sister. On the last day of our stay in Wellington Ajay Singh hosted a lunch for all his friends in Wellington at the residence of another close friend of his, Dinah Priestly. It was here I met Sir Anand and Lady Susan Satyanand for the second time in less than a week. The invitees included a couple of Fiji based families now living in New Zealand, as well as Anna Cottrell and her husband, and Mr. Peter Adams, a Kiwi diplomat, and his wife Monika (sister of Ratu Joni).

During my discussions with Ajay Singh on the book we decided we would request Sir Anand to write its foreword. Only the first draft of the book was ready when I requested Sir Anand and he very kindly sent his text much before the book was sent to the press. He deserves our great admiration and thanks for the same.

Sometime in the middle of May, Ajay Singh had gone to meet Kunwar Natwar Singh ji and shared with him his ideas about the book he was writing on Fiji. He told him that he has already completed two of its chapters and was working on the draft of the remaining ones. Who can understand the value and importance of the biographical writings of a former politician and diplomat other than KNS. He advised Ajay Singh 'to concentrate on finishing his book by putting everything else aside'. He was very much saddened to learn about the passing away of Ajay Singh a few days later. In a telephonic conversation with me he enquired about the status of the book Ajay was writing. On my telling him that I was looking into his notes and hopefully it would be organised. He wailed, "What a pity Ajay did not live to complete the book." My special thanks are due for his constant interest in the book and regular enquiries that encouraged me to expedite the work and finish it early.

Shiromani's sister, Vijaylakshmi Dutt, was kind enough to provide the wedding pictures of Shiromani with Ajay Singh, some of which feature in this book. I also enjoyed her hospitality in Auckland during my brief sojourn to New Zealand with Ajay Singh.

Among the main others who assisted in various ways in the completion of this work, special mention must be made of Mr. Raj Sharma, Amarpal Singh, a long time associate of Ajay Singh and my daughter Mihika. Mihika was one of the few who had received the first version of the first two chapters from Ajay Singh to comment on his writing style and its content. Mihika later made many critical suggestions on the text. My son Navneet and his wife Priyanka also helped me as and when required. Bhuvaneswari, my wife, was very keen that this book should see the light of day as the most fitting tribute to the memory of 'Bhaiyaji' as she used to call Ajay Singh.

Thanks are also due to all sincere well wishers of Ajay Singh who have been anxiously waiting for this book. Dr. A P Singh, a family friend and legal adviser from Australia, kept me ringing at frequent intervals to know its progress, as did Rajinder Panwar, L S Chahar, Dr. Sunita Kuntal from Jaipur and a couple of others.

Finally, I thank Mr. D. Kumar of Shipra Publications for bringing out this volume under harsh corona pandemic conditions. I appreciate his professional acumen and uncompromising nature with quality.

However, for the book's shortcomings, if any, none of the above are responsible.

Introduction

This is my story; the story of my love for the Fiji Islands, its people and of one person in particular. This story begins in 1885 with the epic voyage of my great grandparents across three mighty oceans to a country known as the Fiji Islands, over 19,000 km away from their village near Agra. Their story is also that of the ancestors of all people of Indian origin residing in far away countries like Guyana, Mauritius, Trinidad and many others. It is the story of a new form of slavery disguised in legal trappings, known in history as the Indentured Labour System, under which these hapless people were taken to far away British colonies.

My grand-parents came back to India but my Fiji-born grandfather returned in 1909 to join the Fiji Colonial Civil Service. His experience ran parallel to the rising nationalism in the colonised nations of Asia and the Middle East. With the return of Mahatma Gandhi to India in 1916, the demand for the abolition of the infamous Indentured Labour System became part of the initial demands of the freedom movement. After all, Mahatma Gandhi had honed his tactics of *ahimsa and satyagraha* while fighting for the rights of Indentured Labourers in South Africa. This is how Fiji, as one of the Indian diaspora countries, became an integral part of India's freedom struggle.

My grandfather's civil service record, as preserved in thick files at the Fiji National Archives, tells the tale of his fight to uphold his dignity as an Indian in a racist and colonised society. My father, Bhagwan Singh, born in India, had a distinguished career in the army and the civil service and was an Additional Secretary in the Commerce Ministry when the Prime Minister, Mrs. Indira Gandhi, appointed him as India's first High Commissioner to Fiji in 1971 soon after the nation attained its independence. He had a highly successful five year tenure as the Indian High Commissioner in Fiji. His immense popularity in Fiji was recognised not only by his own government but also by the great council of chiefs of Fiji when they presented him with the sacred Tabua, the highest traditional honour bestowed on an individual; a honour never before bestowed to a non-Fijian.

I had been a witness to the deep bonds my father had with the peoples of Fiji when I stayed with him for almost a year in 1973, and later whenever

I visited him from neighbouring New Zealand where I was studying. Some 34 years later, I was to follow his footsteps as the Indian High Commissioner to Fiji. Dare I say I was full of trepidation and apprehension that I would always be compared to him and found wanting.

Lost in my own anxieties, I had forgotten my *muse,* friend, companion, soul mate and partner for over 35 years: Shiromani Tiwari Singh, nee Shiromani Maharaj, my late wife. Her school alumni network was a huge asset for us as she stood with me shoulder to shoulder in the execution of my duties as the High Commissioner. She brought to a full circle my love story with Fiji.

During my first meeting with my successor, Prof. Prabhakar Jha, he paused mid-sentence and said: "*Arrey Bhai* Ajay Singhji, I have been here for a year now. There have been many High Commissioners of India posted here but the people of Fiji only remember you and your father." Coming from my successor I take it as the ultimate praise for what Shiromani and I had achieved in Fiji!

Allow me now to introduce myself in some detail before I get back to why I decided to write this book. I schooled at Delhi's Modern School as a boarder as my father, who was in the Indian Administrative Service (IAS) and moving around. And it was in school that I made some lifelong friends and developed a taste for English poetry, history and literature as also for smoking, drinking beer and sneaking away with friends to watch movies in nearby Regal Cinema in Connaught Place. I also made my name as a sportsman, particularly in watersports, and was the captain of the school's swimming team.

Post school, I did my BA, with Honours in English, from St Stephen's College, Delhi University in 1971. The college is best known for its significant contribution to the nation's Who's Who in many fields, most notably in governance and industry, but for reasons too complex to go into, I gravitated towards the many bright minds who were part of the extreme Left group then known as Naxalites.

Post college, I hitch-hiked through the Middle East, Eastern and Western Europe, and the USA and finally landed up in New Zealand in 1973. In 1974 I did my post-graduation from the School of Journalism, University of Canterbury in Christchurch and then briefly worked as the Publicity and Promotions Officer for TVNZ1, the national television channel owned and operated by the state owned broadcaster, Television New Zealand. In 1976

I moved to Fiji Islands where I worked as a Senior Sub-Editor for *Fiji Times*, the oldest and largest selling English daily in the South Pacific. In December of that year, I returned to India to join *Surya India*, a monthly magazine. Its editor was the late Khushwant Singh; I and the young Maneka Gandhi were his two senior assistants.

In April 1977 Aroon Purie hired me as a Senior Correspondent to lead the young editorial team of *India Today*, a fledgling fortnightly news magazine he edited. Those were epochal times in Indian journalism. Barely a month ago, the Janata Party had been voted to power, defeating the Indira Gandhi-led Congress, after Mrs. Gandhi had unexpectedly ended the Emergency and called the elections. Our team members were all in their mid-twenties as, indeed so was I, and we were all privileged and excited to be there at the beginning of a new and exciting era in Indian journalism.

However, I left *India Today* in 1978 to take over as Deputy Editor in charge of *Morning Echo*, an English tabloid daily brought out by the Hindustan Times Group. This job was a comparative breeze, and, looking back, was perhaps most memorable for the great times with the inimitable Chand Joshi, legendary journalist and an even more legendary figure at the Press Club, the then favourite watering hole of Delhi journalists.

The good times, so to say, came to an end in March 1980 when I quit HT to take over as the Managing Trustee of the Kisan Trust, set up by Mr. Charan Singh, better known as Chaudhary Charan Singh. Chaudhary Sahib, as we all called him, had been the prime minister till Mrs. Gandhi rode back to power in January 1980. I knew him only slightly but he was good friends with my father.

One day I received summons from Chaudhary Sahib to meet him at his 12, Tughlaq Road residence. One of the key objectives of the All-India Kisan Trust, he explained, was to create an alternative media platform which would speak the language of the peasants and poor people of India, and he was looking for a young, bright and educated person to look after the trust and its publications. I was candid with him about our differing world views since I still held extreme leftist beliefs and I was sure he would revisit his intention of hiring me as the Managing Trustee.

However, I had not taken into account his deeper insights into human psychology, drawn from his long years in public life. He was confident I would look beyond my idealism and come around. Some days later,

I found him sitting with my father at our residence, Tamavua, in Vasant Vihar, Delhi. It was here he asked my father to hand over his only son (me) to him and, in return, take his only son Ajit Singh, a computer engineer who had returned from the United States and joined the DCM Group of Industries. After his retirement, my father was working as an Advisor with Sri Ram Fibres, part of the DCM group. Clearly the elements had conspired to persuade me to quit Hindustan Times and join the Kisan Trust.

When I shared my decision with my media friends, most notably M J Akbar and S P Singh, they were horrified. And when I met K K Birla, the chairman of the company, he too tried to dissuade me: "Ajay you are a young man and doing well in your job. Here you have the opportunity to move up as Editor soon. Politicians come and go. There is a bright future for you in the media. You as Editor will be respected much more by the politicians and they will be approaching you. But outside you will be moving behind them." I told Birlaji politely to accept my resignation and relieve me as I had made up my mind.

It was thus that I became the Managing Trustee of the Kisan Trust, and the Editor-in-Chief of its three media offerings: *Real India*, an English fortnightly, and *Asli Bharat*, a weekly broadsheet in Hindi and Urdu. Chaudhary Sahib was, of course, the Trust's chairman and its trustees were all nationally known figures: Devi Lal, Madhu Limaye, George Fernandes, Biju Patnaik, Sharad Yadav, Ram Vilas Paswan and Dr. Swarup Singh, ex Vice-Chancellor of Delhi University. Interacting with this stellar set of leaders was a deeply learning experience.

Post my association with Chaudhary Charan Singh, my rise in politics was rapid. In 1986 I was elected as a member of the legislative council in UP. After Chaudhary Sahib's death in May 1987, I was unanimously voted by the trustees to replace him as the Chairman of the Kisan Trust. In 1989 I won from the Agra parliamentary seat as a member of Mr. VP Singh's Janata Dal Party and joined the Union Council of Ministers in the short-lived Government led by Mr. Singh, as Deputy Minister in the Ministry of Railways. During the post government period I chaired various government autonomous bodies. Finally In 2005, I was appointed as India's High Commissioner to Fiji, Tonga, Tuvalu and the Cook Islands, the circumstances of which I detail later in the book.

I am retired now, sporadically contributing to various journals and newspapers in India and abroad. With my four-decade long association in journalism, politics, governance, diplomacy and social work I do not lack subjects on which I have something original and relevant to say. These subjects include the non-Congress politics of the Janata Parivar, my experience of working closely with two Prime Ministers of the country, Chaudhary Charan Singh and VP Singh, and my interactions with the big movers and shakers of contemporary Indian politics.

I also head and participate in some social organisations, one of which is the All India Sarv Jat Mahasabha, of which I am the President. I have long been deeply aware that there is much unsaid about the contribution of this community of over 120 million, comprising mainly farmers in Punjab, Haryana, Rajasthan and west UP, to the national weal. People know about the history of the better known heroes of this community, like Maharaja Ranjit Singh, Maharaja Surajmal, Sir Chhotu Ram, Sardar Bhagat Singh, Raja Mahendra Pratap and Chaudhary Charan Singh. But there are innumerable unknown or little known Jat heroes in the armed forces, sports, scientific community, academia and agriculture and even from the freedom movement whose stories have never been told. Thus inclined, I did try to write The Untold History of Jats, but in vain.

Finally, I decided that the book I would write would be on Fiji, spurred on by my two muses. First, and foremost, was my late wife Shiromani who in the last decade of her life had begun to badger me, "Write, my love, write. What a waste it would be if you don't! You have had the unique privilege of working closely with some of the greatest in Indian politics, and had some truly great journalists as friends. So, write...". Seeing me spending hours in my study, she would often say, "You read so much, you know so much, you have stories to tell, on top of it you write so well, it will all be such a waste if you don't...." I wish now that I had written this book when she was alive; she would have plugged gaps in my memory and introduced much colour that will now sadly be lacking.

Second, was my dearest friend from school and college, Aman Nath, the owner of the Neemrana group of hotels. When I left for my odyssey around the globe in 1972, he had given me a heavy, hard-bound volume of blank pages, in which he wrote: "You want to wake those weed grown roads of the past into a song of sable words.... The cleavage you knife, pores of paper and fills it with its royal blood.... So, write." Now, Aman lent his whole-hearted support to Shiromani's urgings to write my book.

Why Fiji First?

I have deep personal knowledge, stretching back four decades, about the island nations of the South Pacific, particularly Fiji, Tonga and New Zealand. And since my family's association with Fiji goes back four generations, spanning almost the entire history of the people of Indian origin in those islands, I have developed deep friendships and have extensive and strong connections with the people there of Indian origin. Indeed it is where I found my love, Shiromani, who was born and brought up in Fiji, and where we got married in 1976.

My wife, Shiromani Maharaj, is a third generation person of Indian origin in Fiji. Our parents had become friends during my father's tenure as the Indian High Commissioner and our families drew even closer with our relationship. The Maharaj family is one of the more prominent families of Fiji; very active in the Shree Sanatan Dharam Organisation, in business and philanthropy. Not surprisingly, her roots go deep into Fiji's 'who's who". Three of her close friends from St Joseph's Secondary School in Suva went on to become the wives of Fiji's President, Home Minister and Defence Minister. They, and their husbands, have also been my friends for almost four decades.

My father had also developed very close personal bonds with the late His Majesty King Taufa'ahau Tupou IV of Tonga who died in 2006. His Majesty's young teenage children were regular guests at our home, "India House" in Fiji. These visits are still remembered by them. We continue to share a warm personal relationship with the present King of Tonga, HRH King George Tupou V, and his popular and politically powerful sister, HRH Princess Pilolevu. My wife and I were her personal guests during a brief holiday in Tonga in November 2008.

As already mentioned, I worked as a journalist in Wellington before returning to India and my friends from those college and journalism days in New Zealand are today editors, current affairs producers on television channels and members of Parliament. In fact, the former Governor-General of New Zealand, Sir Anand Satyanand, is a close personal friend. Our relationship goes back three generations. His grandfather Sriraman Babu and my grandfather Bere Singh worked together for the Fijian civil service in the early 1900s. My father Bhagwan Singh and Anand's father Dr. Mutyala Satyanand continued the friendship. No doubt their encouragement led us to become "pen friends" when I was about 10 years old.

Thus, my connection with this region, particularly with Fiji, has long been well known in Delhi's corridors of power. Our mission in Fiji was forcibly closed following the first military coup in 1987 and was reopened only in 1999 prior to my being sent there as the High Commissioner in 2005. But, in the interregnum, three prime ministers had sent me there on four occasions to assess the situation in Fiji and report back to them: Mr. VP Singh in 1990, Mr. PV Narasimha Rao in 1992 and 1994, and Mr. IK Gujral in 1997. My reports were appreciated and acted upon and they should be available in MEA files.

The South Pacific, a region little known in India, is a distinct geo-political region of about 14 small, independent island nations. They are all members of the UN and many also of the Commonwealth and each has a valuable vote in these two forums. China increasingly competes with Australia and New Zealand for influence among these countries. I would go so far as to say that perhaps no one in India knows the South Pacific region better than I do.

I

CHAPTER

The Appointment

The results of the Indian General Elections of 2004 came as a big surprise all around; to the losers certainly but more so to the winners. The Atal Behari Vajpayee led National Democratic Alliance government had given the country stability and generally good governance. Except for the major blot of the Gujarat communal killings of 2002, its record was fairly clean. The Kargil war was considered by many as one of its several achievements, as were the nuclear tests.

After the initial hiccup over Congress party President Sonia Gandhi replacing Vajpayee, Dr. Manmohan Singh became India's 13th prime minister. He appointed K. Natwar Singh (KNS) as the Union Minister for External Affairs. A distinguished career diplomat, KNS had resigned from the diplomatic service in 1984 to join politics. He contested the general elections later that year on the Congress ticket and was elected the Lok Sabha member from his hometown, Bharatpur, in Rajasthan. Prime Minister Rajiv Gandhi appointed him as his Minister of State for External Affairs. He served the Gandhi government in this capacity till 1989 till the elections that year when Rajiv Gandhi's Congress party government was defeated and Janata Dal's VP Singh formed the new National Front government.

A few weeks after the Manmohan Singh government had taken over in 2004, I got a call from Dharma Kumar whom KNS had appointed as his Officer on Special Duty (OSD). OSDs are part of a small class of secretarial staff who begin their careers in different ministries and departments but are then inducted into various ministers' personal staff. From this perch, they move on from minister to minister, never returning to their original ministry. Not surprisingly, because of their long association with a particular minister, they form the backbone of the minister's office.

I knew Dharma Kumar well. He had served as my Additional Private Secretary when I was Deputy Minister for Railways in the VP Singh government (1989-90). A few days after the new Lok Sabha was sworn in November 1989, I got a call from Mrs. Natwar Singh. A summon from "Chachiji," (Aunty) as I used to call her, could not be taken lightly. When I reached their 9 Safdarjung Road ministerial bungalow, there was the usual chaos of dismantling and moving out of the official bungalow.

Seeing me, she called out for Kumar. Within minutes a short, smartly dressed man, probably in his early forties arrived. "Yes, Madam," he said. Mrs. Natwar Singh turned to him. "This is Ajay Singh, MP from Agra. He is like family. Very soon he will become a minister in this government. You will then join him and help him. He is a first timer." She looked at me quizzically and I quickly said that since she had said it, the matter could be considered done.

So, when Kumar called that fateful day in early 2005, I knew something big was up. When agitated, Kumar tended to talk in short quick gasping sentences and his otherwise impeccable English allowed some accent of his Malayali origins to creep in. "The Minister would like to see you, sir". What about, I asked. He said that the Minister would prefer to tell me himself. OK, when tomorrow, I asked. "No, no, not tomorrow sir. Today. Please come as soon as you can". Mystified, I said "OK, inform the reception desk". I climbed the grand stairs to the first floor of the Minister's Office in South Block, which is on the extreme left of a long corridor while the Foreign Secretary's office is on the far right.

Kumar was all action, ordering around the half dozen clerical staff in the room. But mostly he was busy on the phone conveying the Minister's wishes to various officers. As an OSD he was the man who controlled the access to the great man! One conversation, which I recall clearly even now, amused me in particular. "When I said the Minister wants those papers today, I mean today not tomorrow and I don't care how you do it but do it. He wants results not excuses. I expect to hear from you within an hour," and he banged down the phone, muttering to himself. I sat there wondering: did he do this for me when he was on my staff. because I had never got any joy from the great Railway bureaucracy!

After about half an hour of watching this circus, the phone buzzer finally rang and putting it down Kumar said, "Let's go". Entering the spacious office I found KNS standing and seeing off a distinguished gentleman. He pointed towards the sofas and I took my seat. Shortly thereafter he came over and being a man of few words, came straight to the point.

"Ajay, I am sending you to Fiji," he began.

The short conversation that followed was in hindsight quite amusing.

Me, "What for? What would you like me to do there?"

KNS, "Be the Indian High Commissioner."

Me, "What? Me! The Indian High Commissioner? Are you serious?" I had a feeling KNS was enjoying himself.

He pulled himself erect and in mock severe tones said, "I am the External Affairs Minister of India. We don't make such statements lightly."

I was still looking at him with an idiotic blank gaze when he suddenly stood up.

"OK Ajay I have work to do. Go home tell Shiromani. I want both of you in Fiji within three weeks. Anything she wants to know about her role she can talk to Hem (his wife, Mrs. Heminder Kaur). There will be a lot of preparatory work before you go. Kumar will fix your first meeting with the foreign secretary who will take it from there. So, get going."

With that he stood up. I had been dismissed. I realised that in less than two minutes I had been transformed from a retired and unemployed politician (a misnomer to many) to a full-time diplomat.

Getting into my car I called Shiro. "When can you come home? Take an hour off. I have just met with KNS and I need to discuss some things urgently." Shiro was then working as Programme Officer with the British government's international development agency, DFID. "I have a lot of work to finish, what's this all about," she wanted to know. "I am being sent as High Commissioner to Fiji," I replied smugly. "Did I hear right? High Commissioner! Are you sitting in the Press Club again, boozing with your friends while I slough my back off in this office? Who in hell would appoint you High Commissioner?" she retorted. "Chacha Natwar," I said and disconnected the phone.

Shiro's office was in New Delhi's Qutub Institutional Area. I knew I had her attention when we both reached home within minutes of each other. I told her of the entire encounter with Chacha Natwar. With her beautiful big eyes opening wide, she kept repeating, "This is unbelievable."

Over dinner she suddenly stopped talking and put both her hands over mine. "Here I am yakking away and I have lost you. Come back to me, partner. I know that look very well, what's troubling you?" she said,

> "Well you know I am a bit nervous about all this. We have both seen my father in action in Fiji. His immense success, his popularity not only with the ruling classes but also with the common Fijians, I will always be compared with him and found wanting," I told her.
>
> "Yes, your father was great but you sometimes put yourself down too much. You have your own strengths and don't forget many of our friends from that time, with whom we spent all those weekends and parties, they are people of substance there. And don't forget I am with you and I am a Fiji girl. Between us we will make a great success of your new assignment, believe me."

In our 40-year relationship, she had always been a huge support for me.

Neither of us slept that night.

Next day at 10 sharp I was in Kumar's office. Soon KNS arrived and immediately sent for me, "I presume you have spoken to Shiromani (even he knew who was the boss), and are all set to go. Our man has been there since the Mission reopened five years ago. He needs to be replaced," he said.

I answered: "Yes, Shiromani is submitting her resignation today. There may be a hitch about her contract needing a month's notice, but she is confident she'll manage it."

I went on "Actually Chachaji, since you are appointing ambassadors, why not send me to New Zealand instead of Fiji?"

KNS was a bit taken aback and puzzled. "Why New Zealand?" he asked.

I responded, "Well you know I studied at the post graduate school of journalism at the University of Canterbury. Later I spent a year working for television in Wellington. My classmates are editors and hold important positions in media and in politics. One of them is a member of parliament. I have wide contacts, and know the history, culture and people of that country. In Fiji I will forever be compared to my father, who was a giant."

He was silent for a while. Then he said firmly "For New Zealand I will have to take the matter to the Cabinet. For Fiji, you have a record. Three different prime ministers have sent you incognito to report back to them on the situation there since the military coup of 1987, when our mission there was closed. In fact, all your suggestions to Inder Gujral were carried out, including the suggestion to reopen the mission."

"So, it's Fiji and now we both have work to do," he snapped, and again I had been dismissed from the august presence.

I went home, sat reminiscing on my earlier times in Fiji and the subsequent trips I had made to that country. I realised KNS was correct. Ever since the 1987 coup in Fiji, which had thrown Indo-Fiji relations into a tailspin, I had been the government's go-to "Fiji Expert" recognised by no less than three Indian Prime Ministers.

Shortly after the first military coup in Fiji in May 1987, led by Lieutenant Colonel Sitiveni Rabuka which was, in the main, an act of retribution by the native Fijian community against the dominance of parties representing the large Indian community in Fiji (more on this later), the new regime in Fiji had expelled the Indian High Commissioner, T P Sreenivasan, and the Indian High Commission was closed down. The vast property of India House was entrusted to the General Manager of the Life Insurance Corporation of India and the Indian presence in Fiji was essentially reduced to the Fiji branches of LICI, Bank of Baroda and New India Assurance Co, all public sector entities. Since then, three prime ministers have sent me on four occasions to Fiji to report back on the situation in Fiji. On all occasions, I was to travel as an innocent tourist visiting family and friends.

How these visits happen bear telling. Sometime after the V.P. Singh government was formed in 1989, I learnt that Deputy Prime Minister Chaudhary Devi Lal (who was also Minister for Agriculture) was going to Sydney to attend a two-day conference of Commonwealth Agriculture Ministers. The possibility of a trip to Sydney and maybe a quick side visit to New Zealand and Fiji got me fired up. I had some family and many friends that I wanted to visit. After the 1987 military coup there was an avalanche of Fiji citizens who had migrated to Australia, New Zealand and other accepting countries.

So the very next day I joined Prime Minister VP Singh as he got up to leave the Lok Sabha. I walked with him to his office in Parliament House.

I said to him: "I have just learnt that Devi Lalji is going to Sydney next month to attend some conference. As you know, he has never stepped foot out of India. He is going abroad for the first time in his…", I began.

VP Singh suddenly perked up and cut me mid-sentence. "Yes, yes, I know. I was a bit worried. That's it. You go with him as a chaperone. You have lived in those parts and you know."

Within minutes I had what I was hoping for. The Honourable Member of Parliament from Agra was nominated as an official member of the delegation. It was a three-day trip: day one the conference, day two some local interaction and sightseeing and day three a half hour courtesy call on the Australian Prime Minister Bob Hawke.

A few days after my conversation with Prime Minister VP Singh, External Affairs Minister, IK Gujral spotted me having coffee with some friends in the Central Hall in Parliament. The Central Hall is the circular chamber at the core of the circular Parliament building meant for joint meetings of the Lok Sabha and the Rajya Sabha. It is where idle members of both Houses intermingle with accredited journalists and former members of Parliament. It has been a place of bonhomie, gossip and relaxation over tea and snacks with the very opponents you were fiercely debating inside the House. "Come over to my office this afternoon, I want you to do something," Minister Gujral said.

Around 3 pm that afternoon I drove to South Block and climbed the grand staircase to Mr. Gujral's office. Little did I know then that I would be in and out of that office several times over the next decade and a half.

He came straight to the point. "I have learnt that you are accompanying Chaudhary Sahib to Sydney. I want you to extend your visit and go over to your sasural (parents-in-law's home), Fiji, and bring me back a complete picture of what is happening there, developments, atmosphere, likely developments etc. But you will be going in your private capacity, visiting friends and family."

"It will be strictly private," he said and repeated "private" twice.

Over the next decade I was to make three more such trips to Fiji. In 1992 and 1994, although I was still active in opposition politics as a member of the Janata Dal party, I was summoned by the ruling Congress party Prime Minister P.V. Narasimha Rao and sent on similar journeys. On every occasion the PM needed inputs to help him decide on the vexing Fiji question at a forthcoming Commonwealth Heads of Government meeting.

As part of the international sanctions against the 1987 military coup, Fiji had been expelled from the Commonwealth with India leading the demand for expulsion. Fiji was keen to return to the Commonwealth, not only for practical purposes but also for very emotional reasons. Not only was Fiji cut off from all sorts of aid and beneficial Commonwealth programmes, more importantly it was also cut off from the Crown, the Queen of Great Britain.

The import of that severance becomes evident when you recall that Fiji was the only country in history to voluntarily cede itself in 1874 to the "great white mother", as Queen Victoria was known in the British colonies, as it sought to become part of her fast expanding empire and to come under her protection. It was thus that both the ruling elite of Chiefs and the 'commoner' in Fiji had a deep emotional attachment to the British Crown.

I consider my last such trip in 1997 to be the most crucial. Now IK Gujral was the prime minister. He was scheduled later that year to attend the usual biennial Commonwealth Heads' summit in Vancouver. His instructions to me were the same as when he first sent me to Fiji several years ago. And he also knew that startlingly sweeping changes had taken place since I had last gone to Fiji some three years ago.

Major reconciliatory moves had occurred between the coup leader of 1987 and now Prime Minister, Sitiveni Rabuka, and those he had overthrown a decade ago. The two leaders of the parties which spoke for the Fiji Indians, Jai Ram Reddy, the leader of the National Federation Party, and Mahendra Pal Chaudhary, leader of the Fiji Labour Party, had also shown great statesmanship to make this possible. A new Constitution, more equitable to the Fiji Indians, had been passed and adopted unanimously by Fiji's Parliament.

So, once again the question was: What to do about Fiji? On my return my suggestions were to, firstly, welcome the new Constitution and the ongoing reconciliation process in Fiji. Secondly, I advised that instead of stalling or opposing the return we should ourselves propose that Fiji rejoin the Commonwealth and, thirdly, we should reopen India's mission in Suva. Finally, I said that India must insist that Fiji establish a mission in Delhi.

To back the four initiatives I suggested that the Indian mission return to Fiji with an enlarged aid package which should start with increasing the scholarships given by the Indian Council for Cultural Relations (ICCR) to students for higher studies.

So, on reflection, not only did I have the credentials but I was the logical choice to be appointed High Commissioner to Fiji - the whiff of nepotism notwithstanding. Besides, KNS also knew the formidable difference Shiro would make to my assignment. Shiro too had been dealing with the external affairs ministry, particularly the ICCR, on Indo-Fiji relations.

The task of selecting candidates for Indian government scholarships and organising their travel to India was handled by the Girmit Council of Fiji, the apex organisation of the Indian community in Fiji. Shiro acted as the liaison between the Girmit Council in Fiji and the ICCR in Delhi, sometimes taking time off work to visit the ICCR office for meetings. She was among those recognised in External Affairs Ministry circles for help and advice on dealing with issues relating to Fiji.

Our High Commission was reopened in 1999, a dozen years after its ignominious exit. I was being sent to replace the man who had re-established it there. I knew the incumbent well as he had served as First Secretary and Director of ICC in the Fiji High Commission when my father, Bhagwan Singh, was High Commissioner to Fiji in the mid 70s.

In the Ministry, I was briefed by the Secretary East, Rajiv Sikri and Joint Secretary South, Biren Nanda. This was very fortunate for me because I found them amongst the ablest of officers even as the external affairs ministry had to contend with a sorry lot of bureaucrats. Along with Fiji Islands, I was to be accredited to four Pacific island nations: The Republic of Fiji, the Kingdom of Tonga, Cook Islands and Tuvalu.

We had just moved into our own dream house in Gurgaon that Shiro had built with my childhood friend, the renowned architect, Rasik Bahl. Halfway through setting it up she was having to start packing. The problem of what to do with the house itself was solved in a chance encounter with Julian Moti, a relative of a close family friend, the venerable Sir Moti Tikaram of Fiji. Julian was a Queen's Counsel based in Sydney on an assignment in India. He agreed to take the house on rent and had a peaceful stay in our house in Gurgaon.

The protocol in these ambassadorial change-overs is for the incumbent to be informed of his recall. He then receives a letter which he is supposed to forward to the host government informing it of the new appointment. It is after this is formally accepted by the host government that the new appointee can arrive. I was later told that my predecessor kept delaying this on the pretext of "I want to hand this over personally to the PM"! Finally, the External Affairs Ministry set a firm date for the handing over and for our departure for Fiji.

The Minister's impatience convinced me that he might be worried that if the news of my appointment got to his many political opponents then, knowing of my relationship with him, they might portray the appointment to Mrs. Sonia Gandhi as a case of nepotism and his plans would run into rough waters.

A small digression to the story to give perspective to why it may have been possible, even if remotely, to level the charge of nepotism in my appointment.

It was true that KNS and I were related but it was a very, very distant relation: five times removed. More importantly, KNS was a friend of my father and used to call him *Bhaiji* (elder brother).

But my relationship with KNS really evolved after I joined former prime minister Chaudhary Charan Singh's Kisan Trust as its Managing Trustee in early 1980. It was then that I rediscovered my own cousin, Yadunath Singh, a close associate of Chaudhury Charan Singh. Yadunath, some years older than me, was already a veteran in Rajasthan politics and an MLA from Charan Singh's Lok Dal party from Nadbai constituency in Bharatpur district.

My background and Yadu's could not have been more different even though we were part of the same extended family. Yadu was born in Kasganj, near Nadbai, later to become his Assembly constituency and, from an early age was immersed in rural politics with the interplay of the lives and culture of the area's major dominant castes: the Jats, Yadavs and Gujjars. It was a world to which my real introduction came only through the pages of *Asli Bharat*, the Hindi weekly brought out by the Kisan Trust, and which I edited.

I grew up as a textbook representative of the elitist urban *angrezi-culture wallah*: son of a top civil servant, educated at Modern School and St. Stephen's College, higher studies in a New Zealand university; a member of the Delhi Gymkhana Club, with a residential address in tony Vasant Vihar.

Yadu's world was a whole new world for me. I had much to learn from my cousin and he in turn from me. Over the years we became the closest of friends. Along with much else that we shared we had our absolute devotion to the great Lord Bacchus. Over the years this devotion inspired political gossip. Our leader, Charan Singh, had zero tolerance of anyone who imbibed 'spiritual' stuff.

It was primarily through Yadu that I grew closer to KNS and his wife over the years. As my ties with the Natwar Singhs deepened over the years, I too, like cousin Yadunath, began calling the Natwar Singhs, Chacha and Chachi. Therein, too, lies a story -- or two.

In 1984 KNS, a career diplomat, resigned as secretary external affairs ministry to fight the incumbent general elections. Legend has it that when he told Prime Minister Indira Gandhi of his decision to join politics, he added "And now I am first going to retire all my suits and acquire some khadi kurta pyjamas". Mrs. Gandhi is supposed to have replied, "Natwar, acquire a thicker hide instead, it will be more useful in politics."

In the 1989 general elections, KNS was fighting from Mathura as the Indian National Congress candidate while I was contesting on the ticket of the opposing Janata Dal party from the contiguous Agra constituency. After campaigning through the day, KNS, I knew, was in the habit of returning to Govind Niwas Palace, his home in Bharatpur, hardly 40 kms away from Mathura. My constituency Agra ended where his began.

One night after a days' long electioneering, I found myself in Fatehpur Sikri. Leaving all my supporters behind to rest and disperse, I drove my Maruti Gypsy to Govind Niwas in Bharatpur, an hour's drive, taking along three trusted friends. After all, I was going to visit the "enemy". KNS was then staying mostly at a resort inside the famous Keoladeo Ghana Bird Sanctuary, to avoid the crowds milling around his Bharatpur house round the clock.

It was after dinner time but KNS had still not returned. After a few preliminaries, I sought to take leave of Mrs. Natwar Singh. But she took me into one of the inner rooms and we began discussing each other's campaigns. It was my first election. When I told her that I didn't think KNS was doing too well, she readily agreed. In her uniquely fiery way, she railed at groups and individuals in the area who had switched sides (to my side actually). According to her sources, particularly in the Jat community, I was going to do well, and could "also win, but Natwar is not".

Then she asked how I was for finances. When I replied not well at all, she picked a thick packet wrapped in saffron cloth and handed it to me. The packet contained cash donations from a group of local villagers. In her typical casually regal manner she said, "Take this, it might be of some help." KNS had still not arrived so I declined dinner (although all were starving!) and bid adieu.

As soon as we were out of the sanctuary, I asked one of my companions to have a look at the packet. It was 20,000 rupees in soiled notes of small denomination. We just could not believe it and counted it over several times to confirm the sum. I felt humbled with her gesture of generosity and support. From then on I began, like Yadu, calling them Natwar Chacha and Hem Chachi.

Hence, I understood that even though I was not a close relative, the charge of nepotism could stick to my appointment.

The weeks prior to departure was a daze of packing for Shiro, and official meetings for me. I also had to formally call on Prime Minister Manmohan Singh whom I had never met. In his usual polite manner, Dr. Manmohan Singh rose to greet me and said, "I am glad it's you who is going. I used to know your late father; he was a good friend. He was referred to by many as Mr. Fiji."

It was followed by a courtesy call on the Leader of the Opposition, L.K. Advani, whom I knew from my political days. Advaniji was fascinated by my Fiji story and said "I never knew your connection to Fiji. So, you are the fourth generation going there. I only saw your political avatar," he added.

In early February I was finally handed over my scroll of credentials. Above a large embossed stamp, on parchment paper it read:

> "Great and Good friend,
>
> Being desirous of maintaining and strengthening cordial relations, which exist between our two countries, I have decided to accredit to Your Excellency, as High Commissioner, Ajay Singh, a distinguished citizen of India. The qualities, which distinguish him, assure me of the care he will take to acquit himself of the high mission, which is entrusted to him so as to obtain Your Excellency's confidence and thus merit my approbation. It is in this conviction that I request Your Excellency to receive him with your usual graciousness and to attach faith and complete credit to all that he will say to you on my behalf and especially when he will convey to Your Excellency the assurances of my high esteem and my constant friendship."

This was issued by the President of India Dr. A P J Abdul Kalam on February 4, 2005 with his seal embossed on it.

In my study at home I have a copy of this scroll framed next to another, issued 34 years ago to my father by President Varahagiri Venkata Giri. A rare case in Indian diplomatic history of a son following his father as ambassador to the same country.

Citizenship of Shiro

Amidst all the preparations, I was asked by the Ministry to provide three passport size photos of Shiro and myself for issuance of diplomatic passports.

Stuck in one of Delhi's perennial traffic jams, Don McLean singing "America Pie" in the background, a thought struck me with the force of a sucker punch: Shiro and her damned blue Fiji passport!

For me her insistence in retaining it had been a pain for the past three decades. A pain because her residency visa had to be renewed every three years. In our initial struggling days, it was worse because we would invariably forget to renew it till it was too late. And suddenly one day, with the deadline virtually on our heads, we would awake to the need for its renewal.

Then I would have to run around locating a "contact" who would help us work around the delay and the accompanying hefty fines condoned or waived. The trip to the ever-changing addresses of the Foreigner's Registration Office of the Ministry of Home Affairs used to be a two to three-day exercise. But love is blind and I deeply respected her sentiments.

The only time I had ever raised the issue was when I was elected to the Lok Sabha in 1989. Holding important parliamentary positions in the ruling National Front alliance and in the the Janata Dal, I was widely expected to be inducted into the Union Council of Ministers.

Inching forward towards the red light, stuck in Delhi's traffic, I replayed that scene in early 1990 when I had raised the issue. We were sitting in our living room, nursing a pre arrival-of-guests drink when Shiro joined me combing her thick knee-length hair. I began circuitously, talking about the significance of being the sole General Secretary of the ruling Front as well as the ruling party and how soon I could be a minister in our government. I even talked about how I wish the PM would give me a portfolio where I could do some developmental work for our constituency etc. She would once in a while add her bit to this short monologue.

Eventually I began. "Well Shiro, in all these developments, I was thinking of your Fijian citizenship. Everybody from the PM to leaders of the Opposition as well as the media know you. And I must say, it helps a lot that you are popular with them all, the seniors and others (my feeble attempt at softening her!), but no one knows you are not an Indian citizen. With your Indianness, your popularity, no one even thinks otherwise.

"But if it were to ever come out, that the wife of this rising star, this soon to be Minister already holding important parliamentary positions, is a foreigner who has not chosen Indian citizenship in all these year, it could be very embarrassing for us. Remember what happened to Sonia Gandhi and the ruckus over the delay in her acquiring Indian Citizenship."

The smooth flow of the hairbrush came to an abrupt stop. Her beautiful big eyes became bigger as she gazed at me steadily for a while. "I gave up my home, my family, my country for you and now you want me to give up my very identity. I am a third generation Fijian, born and brought up in Fiji. But I am more Indian than many of our Indian friends and you often acknowledge that. But my identity is Fijian and I always thought you understood. Now you want me to erase that just because of your politics and what others may say!" She stood up.

I tried a different tack, blundering into making a reference to her ancestors. "Shiro, what are you getting so heated up about? Your identity is also of the Sanatan Dharam. Your father was the founding President of the Shri Sanatan Dharam Sabha of Fiji and remained President till his death in 1979. And according to Manusmiriti, a wife has to adopt the *gotra* of her husband."

"Well, it's just not going to happen, so piss off. And try staying sober, specially with this gang of wine lovers coming tonight," she stormed off to get ready.

I had replayed this nightmare several times by the time I reached home. I was aware that this time the question of Shiro's nationality would not die down so easily. But I also realised it would be futile to raise it with her.

Next day, I laid my problem at KNS' feet. He thought for a moment and said, "Well if it is so important to her I can sanction it, but I don't think she realises the embarrassment it would be for her. Let me talk to her." I buzzed Kumar on the telecom to get Shiro on the line at home. "I'm with Chachaji, he wants a word with you about that passport thing," and I handed the receiver to KNS.

"Namaste Shiromani. I didn't know but Ajay just told me that you still hold your Fiji passport. Since he tells me you have rather strong feelings about it, I suppose under my powers I could sanction it. But you are going to your Fiji. While you may sit together in the aeroplane, once out, he will be in the VIP diplomatic protocols and you in the general lines. Awkward, embarrassing situations could occur for you. Think it over and decide. Either way, it is OK with us."

Entering home that evening the atmosphere struck me with the force of a Delhi *aandhi.* I felt enveloped in the eerie atmosphere which one would find at a family bereavement. Not getting a reply, I slowly climbed the stairs towards the TV lounge. Shiro was sitting on the floor, stuff strewn around. I ventured: "How are things? What's up?"

The response was short: "Can't you see? Packing."

Taking the hint I stammered "Well, you carry on, I am not very hungry, maybe some soup and a sandwich. I have papers from the ministry to be returned tomorrow."

In her curt dismissal she said "So, tell Dalip (the long time cook and Man Friday) and do what you have to."

I made a hasty descent to my study. Even Dalip was in mourning! Ensconced in my sanctuary with my old friend, Mr. Old Monk rum, along with my older friend Amjad Ali Khan, the sarod maestro classmate from the Modern High School days, playing, I pulled out my new discoveries, a volume each of the Russian poets, Anna Akhmatova and Osip Mandelstam.

I crawled into bed well past midnight and instantly knew Shiro was pretending to sleep. I dozed off. Long after the birds had begun their chirping, a deathly silence hung over the room. At the breakfast table suddenly Shiro said, "I suppose it has to be done, Chachaji clinches it. I am going to see Luke." Picking up her bag and car keys she was gone.

Fiji had recently opened its first High Commission to India at a premise near Hauz Khas. High Commissioner Luke Rokovada had made his first call on Shiro after he presented his credentials. Apparently, he had been Shiro's student in various courses conducted by her as Training Officer in the Fiji Public Service.

After graduating from Miranda House, Delhi University in 1971, Shiro had returned to Fiji and joined the Fiji Civil Service which is equivalent to the Indian Administrative Service. Now in Delhi, Luke and his wife, Vani had quickly become close friends, appointing us patrons and guides on all matters, from domestic help to political, social, economic situation etc. I generously provided him access to the senior bureaucracy and various institutions in Delhi.

Luke later described the scene in his office. What should have been a half hour matter took five hours. When it came to surrendering her passport, Shiro apparently broke down. A panicked Luke sent for his wife Vani who happened to be visiting the office. They eventually took Shiro home and fed her lunch. The nostalgia that went with the kai viti (aboriginal Fiji) food soon calmed her down. I know that 'kokoda', her favourite Fijian delicacy (a raw fish salad which is Fiji's version of ceviche, enriched with coconut milk to balance the acid) would have played a large role in it.

Returning home, she walked into my study to announce: "Well, you in particular will be very happy to know that the deed is done. You can proceed with the passports." She had made her decision and normalcy seeped in achingly over the next several hours like the slowly melting glaciers feeding the Himalayan rivers at their source.

Another day, I suddenly remembered another classmate from school, Sudhir Nayar. His father was the legendary author, journalist and editor, Kuldip Nayar who went to London in 1990 as India's High Commissioner to the UK. I called on Nayar Sahib at his residence to gain some insights about diplomatic assignments and on dealing with the bureaucracy in the Ministry of External Affairs.

The Foreign Service usually looks askance at "political appointees" – the term used for those appointed as ambassadors who are not from the ranks of the Indian Foreign Service. Ambassadorial posts are the preserve of the IFS but the Minister or Prime Minister also may appoint a few ambassadors who are persons of eminence in their field or have a special connection with the host country. My father, though a top civil servant, was also considered an 'outsider' by Foreign Service officers in the Ministry, but with his vast administrative experience and connections, he was able to withstand the MEA establishment. I, however, had much to learn from the veterans.

In particular, I was keen to know about my entitlements. I had heard that the Representational Grant was meant for hospitality and entertainment, and that the Foreign Allowance is the cost of living subsidy indexed to the host country so that an appropriate lifestyle for a diplomat could be maintained in the country of posting.

From Kuldip Nayar, I learnt of another set of allowance which included an "outfit allowance" to buy yourself suits and ties, including the mandatory black *achkan* and churidar pyjamas. After independence, Prime Minister Jawaharlal Nehru had chosen black *achkan* or sari as the dress code for Indian ambassadors when presenting their credentials to the host country's head of state.

Getting my *achkan* stitched became a *shagufa* by itself. It was suggested to me that I should reach out to Chacha Abdul Haq Khan, professor in Jamia Millia Islamia University in Delhi, and a close friend of my father. He insisted on taking me to his personal *darzi* - the renowned tailor M. Hasan of Aligarh, who had served as a tailor to former Presidents Zakir Hussain, Sanjeeva Reddy, V.V. Giri and Fakhruddin Ali Ahmed. A well-fitting *achkan* is a work of art. Chacha Abdul Haq said "*Beta, yeh to perfect honi chahiye. Tum ye nahein samjhoge, mein aaj kitna khush hun.*" (This must be a perfect fit. You would not realise how happy I am today!).

Prof. Abdul Haq's family was known to my father from his days as Collector in Bulandshahr. There were a couple of Zamindar families in that district, both Hindus and Muslim. He belonged to a Muslim Zamindar family of Pathan origin from Barahbasti in Bulandshahr. Chacha Abdul Haq's father-in-law, Abdul Rashid Khan was a prominent lawyer and the Chairman of Bulandshahr's Municipal Body who had established the Degree College of Bulandshahr in 1930.

Chacha Abdul Haq shared sports hobbies with my father. They used to play badminton and hockey in the Montford Club adjoining the residence of the Collector, and they had collaborated to start a sports tournament in the name of my mother Shanta Singh in Bulandshahr. The Captain Bhagwan Singh Sports Stadium in Bulandshahr exists even today as evidence of his love for and promotion of sports by my father in his district of administration.

The Bulandshahr area is also known for its delicious Dussehri mangoes, regarded by its devotees as the king of mangoes. During the mango season, Chacha Abdul Haq used to send baskets full of mangoes to my father and his other friends in Bulandshahr.

This tradition still continues. Till the other day, Emran, the son of Chacha Abdul Haq who is also a professor of Mechanical Engineering in Jamia Millia Islamia University, would suddenly appear at my house in Gurgaon unannounced and would ask his driver, in a very regal manner, to bring in the cartons of mangoes from their ancestral orchard in Bulandshahr. The last time he came, I learnt from him that Chacha Abdul Haq was no more and had passed away in September 2019.

I also found I could claim the "outfit allowance" amount in advance from the ministry. Among the other allowances I discovered was something called the "doormat" allowance, which is meant to cover sundry expenses when you moved into your official residence such as things like door mats!

The couple of hours we spent with Bharati and Kuldip Nayar were to prove more valuable than some of the briefings I was subjected to by the ministry's so-called experts. Sometimes I would sit through these briefings wondering if the person briefing me knew anything beyond the bits he was regurgitating to me from "A Note on Fiji" prepared by some unknown babu in the ministry.

Being a dilliwallah, our circle of friends was larger than most, comprising mates from my school Boarding House, school, sports, college, media, politics along with all of Shiro's friends. It soon became a round of cocktail parties and farewell dinners. I went around telling my friends, "Better come soon to Fiji; the South Pacific is another world with its beautiful island resorts, stunning beaches and unlimited duty-free booze. But come fast because I have a certain *kismet.* I became an MP for five years, and was an ex-MP in 16 months, the shortest Lok Sabha in our history. Then I became a minister and the government collapsed in six months."

Later I reminisced over my father's farewells. How different were those from mine, and I wondered how different our tenures would be. In Agra, our village, Bharatpur, Jaipur, Mathura and of course in Delhi individuals and organisations had vied to host my father in public functions, speeches and private parties.

Shiro was then the sole earner in the family. I existed on my meagre Lok Sabha pension, which covered the essentials including my Press Club subscription, liquor, cigarette and fuel bills. Her VRS Cheque enriched us enough to buy some personal gifts for our large number of friends in Fiji.

The Ministry, besides their briefings, gave some gifts for select VIPS in Fiji and other countries of accreditation.

We called on KNS and his wife the day before our departure. Besides their blessings, KNS's final shot was addressed to Shiro. Pointing to me he told her sternly, "And no boozing!"

Finally, on 28th February 2005 we were on the Air India flight, first class for the first time, and bound for Sydney. We took a few days' stopover to meet family and friends. I made it a point to catch up with Karam Ramrakha, a brilliant lawyer and one of the fiery leaders of the Fiji Indian dominated National Federation Party which was in opposition in Fiji's Parliament. He had retired and set up his legal firm in Sydney. His father, Odin Ramrakha, and my grandfather, Bere Singh had been colleagues and close friends in the early 1900s. Both Ramrakha and my grandfather were among the first Indians to be taken into the Fiji Colonial Civil Service.

His long lunch briefing to Shiro and me were always interesting, especially on the changes in Fiji politics. He spoke of the developments after the Fiji coup of 2000 that dislodged the government of his own rival, Labour Party Prime Minister Mahendra Chaudhary. These briefings were to be invaluable in my early days in Suva.

In parting, Karam could not resist one last dig: "And don't soak those Fijian chiefs in Fiji with whisky like your father used to." Although he and his four brothers called my father, "the eldest Ramrakha" and treated him as one, Karam as a politician was amongst those critical of the rapport and personal relationships my father had developed with all levels of Fijian society, particularly their high chiefs. In the early days after Fiji's independence, the Indians in Fiji saw the Indian High Commissioner as 'their' High Commissioner and did not approve of his mingling with the ethnic Fijians.

We finally arrived in Fiji on March 4, 2005. We made the breathtakingly beautiful descent to the runway at Nadi International Airport. I had made this descent several times over the last 34 years, but that feeling of about-to-land-right-into-the-sea never goes. And the green cloud topped mountains and the verdant sugarcane fields always, always lift your heart.

II
CHAPTER

My Great Grandparent's Tryst with Destiny

My Fiji story starts in a medium-sized village named Jaingara, a few kilometres off the Agra-Fatehpur Sikri highway to Jaipur. It's an ancient village. I was told by the village elders that until recently the family of the traditional priest who looked after the ancient Dauji Mandir had a *tampatra* from an official of Emperor Akbar's reign which granted him a part of the revenue from the neighbouring two dozen villages for the maintenance of the temple.

During the late 1870s, there lived in Jaingara a prosperous farmer called Fateh Gulab Singh. Gulab Singh was a descendent of one of the several petty Jat chieftains whose major pastime during previous generations had been to raid the rich caravans of the Moghul Empresses as they travelled between Delhi and Fatehpur Sikri. The weakened Mughal rulers in their decline had made truce with these petty chieftains by giving them the title of *Faujdars* and allowing them to collect small levies in turn for the safe passage of their caravans

On his death, Gulab Singh's three sons continued to farm his relatively vast property. The elder two, Bansi Bir Singh and Ram Chander Singh, had both married and settled down to farming in accordance with their father's wishes.

Gulab Singh had arranged the marriages of his children according to tradition, when they were still infants. The wife of his second son, Ram Chander, turned out to be someone special, growing up into a fair, charming, beautiful young woman with an equally amiable nature which made her very popular with the old and young alike. Old timers, still living in the village, had heard of her from their parents. They also remembered her as a very religious and devout person.

For some time after their father's death, the three brothers worked his land and lived together. But towards the middle of 1884, Ram Chander left the village accompanied by his wife and her cousin, Narain. The exact reason for this is not known. But it could well have been because of a dispute over the eternal issue of land. Without written wills, the inheritance of land was and still remains a common source of discord in these communities and villages.

In fact, one of the commonest reasons why Indians of the time left their villages and became an easy prey for the indentured labour recruiters was a family dispute regarding land. The younger brothers generally were the ones who suffered the most. Something similar happened in this case too. First it was the youngest member of Gulab Singh's family who took off towards the Himalayas and returned years later as a Sadhu.

Then Ram Chander left behind his share of the land and all his worldly goods and walked out of the village. Whether the motive was dispute over land, the hot-headedness of youth, or that particular craving for adventure in the big wide world beyond will remain a mystery cremated with him. What is definite is that he and his wife, Padam Kaur, and her cousin, Narain, headed for Agra, the big glittering city of the region about 25 km from their village.

An Emigration Depot had been established in Agra and several other cities in the then United Provinces for recruitment of labourers from the neighbouring districts for the expanding British Empire with several colonies in the West Indies, Africa, Mauritius and Fiji. Indian labour was valued because they were more productive and more easily managed than the local natives.

The Indian diaspora's story in Fiji and other dominions of the British Empire begins in 1833, when the British Parliament banned the practice of slavery throughout its rapidly expanding dominions. As the British empire straddled the globe, it acquired strategic but economically unviable countries, particularly on the main sea routes like the Caribbean, Atlantic, Indian and Pacific oceans. To maintain far-flung colonies like Trinidad, Guyana, Mauritius and Fiji it also needed cheap labour.

Having banished slavery from its realms, and keeping the strong public opinion at home against slavery in mind, the empire created a new system for procuring cheap labour: the system of indentured labour. Among the indentured labour, this system came to be known as the Girmit system and those who joined the workforce under this system through an agreement to work in the crown colonies became known as the Girmitiyas. This nomenclature was actually the corrupted form of the 'agreement', which, of course, the illiterate labourers were unable to pronounce.

The emigration of Indians contracted under the "indenture system" commenced in 1837. To appease the moralists the indenture contracts were to be regulated by authorities in India in order to "safeguard" the interests of the emigrants who were supposedly freely recruited with full understanding of their contractual commitments and obligations.

When the first emigrant ship the 'Leonidas" arrived in Fiji on 15th May 1879, it added a further 498 more Indians to the over 340,000 who had been lured over the previous forty years to travel to Natal, British Guyana, Trinidad, the West Indies, and the Dutch, Spanish and French colonies.

Although the seemingly benign and paternalistic officials of the Raj in India felt responsible for the welfare of the migrants, they pragmatically realised that the commercial interests of Great Britain was always the priority. Hence the Indian Emigration Act was an effort, though mostly unsuccessful, to mitigate the more evil aspects of the indenture system.

The policy was decided by the colonial Government of India but its day-to-day implementation was left to officials in the port of Kolkata. When decades later recruitment was extended to the South, Chennai was established as the second port under the charge of a "Protector of Emigrants". Colonies wishing to enter the emigrant market nominated an emigration agent to reside at the port of embarkation and to maintain an approved emigration depot.

The agent in turn, appointed recruiters licensed by the Protector of Emigrants known locally as *arketiyas*. When the Fiji Government came on to the emigrant scene, it appointed one of the two existing government emigration agencies in Kolkata to be their agents. These agencies were shared by Fiji, Trinidad, Jamaica, Mauritius, Grenada, St. Lucia and St. Vincent.

Agra was a much more important city of northern India in those days than it is today. It was a major military cantonment and one of the nerve centres of the British Raj. We must not forget that it had been the seat of the mighty Moghul Empire till just a few centuries earlier. Agra regained its lost importance in 1857 when the British government took over the acquisitions of the unscrupulous East India Company, leading to the creation of the United Provinces (UP) of Agra and Oudh.

In Agra, Ram Chander's destiny took a fateful turn when he met some recruiters from the Government Emigration Agency in Calcutta. The recruiters that Ram Chander met were supreme con artists. They were masters of the promotional medium and the smoothest ad-men of the time. They worked for the sub-agent appointed by the nominated emigration agent of the then Government of Fiji. The sub-agent in turn would issue them licences to recruit emigrants.

Working out of sub-depots established around the country, the recruiters known as 'harkatis' hung around bazaars, 'melas', temples and on the roads just outside the town. Here they would identify the most vulnerable and gullible. It was easy for them to identify and lure the hungry, lost, young villagers desperately trying to find safety in the confusion of the 'big town'.

Ram Chander, his wife and her cousin were easy to spot and a conversation ensued. It began with polite friendly generalities till Ram Chander's frame of mind became evident. Then, slowly, the question of emigration was introduced. As the recruiters unfolded their con deal camouflaged in attractive propositions of security, wealth and certainty Ram Chander's imagination was roused. The offers were seemingly God sent as were the agents. He had begun to trust and even like these men. They were so nice and friendly. They talked of this far away land of immense possibilities in addition to its natural beauty and lushness. These tales of golden opportunities described a country where men could grow rich in a short time and acquire their own piece of land. The many lies included some isolated truths.

Ram Chandar was slowly persuaded. Having formed this glowing image in his mind and after several days of patient smooth-talking from these men who had befriended him in his hour of need, Ram Chander decided to sign on. Thus, Ram Chander became another grain in the sands of time of a new era.

In far away Fiji, this was the era which began with the then Fiji ruler, Ratu Seru Cakobau's decision to cede his country to the great white mother, Queen Victoria in 1874 and her appointment of Sir Arthur Gordon as the new colony's first Governor. Gordon was charged with developing the new colony's economy so that it would not be a burden on Britain. He also had a view that the natives of the new colony should not be exploited and their interests including land holding be protected.

Fiji already had several farmers and entrepreneurs, mainly from Australia trying to make their fortune in sugar and cotton. Their problem was a reliable supply of cheap labour as the native Fijian did not fulfil this need. Gordon had served in Mauritius and knew about the value of Indian indentured labourers. So he saw this avenue as a solution.

For the recruiters Ram Chandar, his wife Padam Kaur and cousin Narain were a rare catch; three birds with one stone. Importantly they were a simple and semi-literate young couple with a relative eager to start a new life. Such recruits were the best as they were least likely to change their minds on the way or cause any problems at the interview with the "protector of immigrants'.

For the recruiters, this recruitment was indeed profitable. The sub-agent would be able to claim a commission of about Rs. 25 each for Ram Chander and Narain, and Rs. 34 for Padam Kaur. Women were highly prized as recruits as the ratio of male to female labourers in the colonies was 4:1. The recruiters, in turn, could claim a third of the sub-agent's commission as their expenses for their efforts.

The recruiters took Ram Chander and his wife to the sub-depot maintained by the sub-agent situated near the famous Red Fort of Agra, once the throne of the Mughal Empire. This was the more sparsely populated section of the city in those days as it had not fully recovered from the ravages of the 1857 war of independence.

The recruits were housed in one of the several ordinary looking barracks that made up the sub-depot. Here Ram Chander and group were given good food and treated with respect and consideration. They were given a routine medical examination by one of the agency's two medical inspectors who made sure their hands had corns as evidence of hard manual labour and that Ram Chander's chest measured more than 32 inches.

(I am grateful to my father Bhagwan Singh for these details, well enumerated in his book, My Father's Land Fiji, and to his biographer Dr. Natthan Singh for his book *Khet Khalihan Se Rajdhani ka Safarnama.*)

After this, they were coached by the recruiters in preparation of their visit to the recruiting officer who was the local Sub-Divisional Magistrate. It was the duty of this officer to ascertain whether the emigrants understood the terms of their agreement and were going of their own free will. Thus, the coaching was done with practised sophistication to preclude the possibility of a thorough examination and to ensure that most would pass.

The officials of the Raj, often Indians at this level, by and large disliked the emigration process and could have asked telling questions which could have led to lengthy enquiries or even outright rejections. Thus the coaching was vital in order to beat the "Protector of Emigrant's" scrutiny.

In Ram Chander's case they need not have worried. The Sahib was busy and asked no frightening questions about "Kalapani". Kalapani was a term sheathed in superstition about the sins attendant to crossing the ocean so as to frighten people planning to leave India. In addition, no questions were asked about his understanding of penal servitude being enshrined in the agreement. Ram Chander and his wife had never been in close proximity to a Sahib, let alone spoken to a European.

For the Sahib they were a young married couple who he could vouch were going willingly. The Sahib formally registered them as emigrants and witnessed their signature to the agreement. Ram Chander signed his name in Hindi using unconnected letters according to the style of the day. His wife, Padam Kaur, did the same.

Both of them, after this, stayed at the Agra sub-depot for a while. As soon as a sufficiently large group had collected, the sub-agent booked them on the train to Calcutta in an ordinary third-class compartment. They were accompanied by some of his assistants as escorts to ensure that no one grew disillusioned and decamped *en route.*

They boarded the train at Agra Fort station. It was a motley group of travellers. Some had been kidnapped, some blatantly forced and others had been persuaded to start the long journey through a shrewd combination of deceptions which included a few truths, many more half-truths and mostly outright lies. Later generation Fiji writers like Brij Lal, K L Gillion, Totaram Sanadhya and Rajendra Prasad etc. have described this process of deception extensively. In any case, the overwhelming majority on the train had no idea of what their journey to paradise was really about. Reality was to strike them only when they were drowning in their despair and escape was not an option.

The trip lasted several days taking them through the major towns of the erstwhile United Provinces, now Uttar Pradesh, Bihar and Bengal before they reached the last stop on the line, the Howrah railway station. On the way, they were fed and looked after by the sub-agent's assistants. For many this experience of regular meals and sustenance was new and reassuring.

The route taken then was the same as any traveller would take today, crossing almost 1300 kilometres of the Gangetic plain passing through Kanpur, Allahabad, Varanasi and Patna. Travelling eastwards, they passed through increasingly impoverished lands. It was this area, east of Allahabad, now renamed Prayagraj, where the majority of their fellow recruits for Fiji would come from. This was largely due to the fact that the creation of a rural proletariat was more advanced in Bihar and the eastern regions of the United Provinces than the rest of India.

Ram Chander's group had been kept apart from the rest of the passengers on the train as well as from the rest of the crowd when the train finally arrived at Howrah station. Although their escorts had managed to prevent anybody from getting close to them during the train journey, there were several cases of railway officials and others jeering at them or trying to persuade them to run away while there was still a chance. Their advice was based on an awareness of the organised deception which had been calculatingly used to exploit the vulnerability of those disempowered by circumstance.

The group's escorts were able to persuade their bewildered wards to ignore the jeers. They were warned by their protectors that the jeering came from people who were either jealous or wanted bribes from them. But these incidents were to occur with a greater frequency and affected the members of the group deeply during their stay in Calcutta.

They got their first taste of it at the Howrah station itself where a crowd gathered around them as soon as word got round that another group of prospective immigrants had come on the train. The crowd taunted and insulted the group's escorts and repeated the dire warning and alarming exaggerations of things awaiting those who migrated. The escorts had anticipated this and had, immediately on arrival, finalized the payment of bribes to various policemen on duty. These bribes varied from four to six annas per recruit in 1885. With time, this bribe amount had to go up considerably as the nationalistic feeling against immigration gathered momentum in India.

The group, escorted by the police and a handful of other people who had attached themselves to the procession, marched over the bridge and then for many kilometres through the streets of Calcutta to the Emigration depot at 61, Garden Reach. Every individual carried his meagre belongings on his back or head. By the time they reached the depot some persons from the group had absconded. They were the ones who had been forced by various means to sign on. The migrations were unpopular. Even the policemen, though bribed, turned a blind eye to the escapees. In later years, to prevent such occurrences, the prospective migrants were taken straight to the depot across the holy river on launches from the station.

Ram Chander, in spite of his growing apprehensions, was still bent upon going. He pushed his doubts into the background and lost himself in the sights, sounds and smells of one of Asia's biggest cities. Calcutta in those days was the 'Jewel of Asia'. The capital of the sprawling sub-continent, known as British India, it was one of the most colourful, vibrant and busy centres of the empire which claimed that it was so vast that the sun never set in it. The vice-regal residence, Fort William, the Maidan, the wide avenues full of bustling, moving crowds of people, animals and ornate 'buggies' added to the splendour of the city. It was a city made fittingly resplendent with the symbols and signs to show the might of British Imperialism.

Ram Chander spent his last few hours as a free man in the wonder and excitement of the world that was Calcutta. But the growing apprehension of his forthcoming journey somewhat tended to dampen his spirits. The first gave him the impression of the big wide world that lay before him but the latter spelt a faintly written warning of what was to come. It would be eight long years before he regained his freedom from his contract and another eight years before he returned to this city and set foot on Indian soil again.

The procession finally arrived at the depot at Garden Reach which was situated on the banks of the Hooghly river. It was an enclosure with spread out grounds, rows of barracks for the emigrants, a hospital, a shed and several other buildings. Once inside the depot, the emigrants were not allowed to go out, but few felt the loss of liberty as it was a happy place for them. They were given little work to do and the food was good. They bathed in the river and spent most of the time getting to know each other. They were well treated here and anyone who had second thoughts and wanted to leave was immediately removed in order to prevent his dissatisfaction spreading to the others. Ram Chander's group had to wait several weeks before they formed a suitably large number for a ship to sail.

The day after their arrival in Calcutta, Ram Chander and his wife were taken along with the others to meet the Protector of Emigrants who visited the depot twice a week. An official again explained the terms of the agreement to the people assembled before the Protector. Then Ram Chander and his wife were taken aside separately and questioned to make sure that they understood what was involved and that they were going out of their own free will. This was a hurried process which was over within five minutes.

The Journey

Towards the end of March 1885, there was great excitement at the depot. The word had spread that since enough people had been collected, they would all be sailing shortly. A ship called the "SS Ganges" was the eleventh indenture ship to sail for Fiji, the previous ten having carried 5,048 people there. It was to be followed by 80 other ships, landing a total of 54,982 Indians on the Fijian shores before the system was abolished in 1916.

Early on 11 April, 1885, a total of 538 men, women and some children left the depot and headed for the Kidderpore docks. At the docks they were supplied with blankets and thick clothing as their ship would be sailing into the chilly and rough weather to the south of Australia. The emigration agent, who had accompanied them to the docks, got busy selecting the cooks, sweepers, cleaners and other workers for the voyage. He also appointed 'Sardars', one for every 25 immigrants, to oversee discipline, cleanliness and general day to day affairs.

The Emigrants Pass Book, volume 23, at the National Archives of Fiji shows that a young married couple, Ram Chander and Padam Kaur (depot Nos. 1589 and 1590), aged 25 and 22 years, belonging to Zila Agra, 'Pargana Fatehpur Sikri, 'Thana' Kerawli and village Jaingara, boarded the "Ganges" towards the end of the migrant queue on 11 April 1885. Accompanying them was Padma Kaur's cousin, Narain.

The "SS Ganges" was a part of the fleet owned by one Mr. James Nourse and was specially fitted out for colonial immigration. A 14,000 tonner, it carried some 550 people and a cargo of rice, dal, spices, furniture, mangoes and mango saplings. The between deck, the upper deck and the poop were reserved for the immigrants. Ram Chander and his wife were in one compartment for married couples while three male members shared other similar compartments. Toilet facilities were at the stern.

With the final count-down over, a tug took the ship down to the mouth of the Hooghly river. There was much commotion, loud chattering, wailing of women and a total absence of well-wishers to wave them off. For Ram Chander the long exile had begun. Like the god whose name was given to him at birth, he set out on his own wanderings. His wife, like Lord Ram's spouse Sita, was with him. For Laxman, they had Padam Kaur's young cousin, Narain. Their exile would last 16, instead of 14, years!

The atmosphere began to cool down by the third day when they reached the Bay of Bengal. Almost no one had seen the mighty ocean before. The biggest expanse of water for them had been the Ganges or the Yamuna Rivers.

Soon everyone began to settle down to the daily routine of the voyage. Ram Chander and his shipmates rose early every morning, tied their belongings into bundles wrapped in blankets and hung them to bamboo poles. They washed and had their breakfast on the upper deck while the ship was being cleaned. In fine weather they stayed there till late afternoon singing, playing cards and amusing themselves. The ration was liberal, the food not bad and they ate sitting in long rows on the deck. The women helped in the kitchen and with other minor work while the men helped in cleaning, washing, drawing water and similar chores. There was plenty of time to get to know each other.

It was a herd of humanity sailing across the seas to "build a new world for themselves, through their own blood and sweat, through the births and deaths of their own hopes and dreams". It was a time of trepidation, of reflection and of dreaming. Some were escaping from their past, others going eager to experience their future. Some were making the voyage resigned to the fact that all that happens is for the best and life's steps can only take one to something.

The immigrants on this voyage were a heterogeneous group, dominated by Brahmins, Thakurs, Ahirs, Chamaars, and a few Muslims. But there was also a Pathan, a Gujjar, and a few Banias, Dhobis, Gowalas (Ahirs, better known as Yadavs) and other castes. There was even a Zamindar!! Besides Ram Chander and his wife, there was another Jat couple with a three-year-old son and three others single Jats.

The long voyage across the kalapani erased their caste as they were now forced to live communally, and more importantly eat together. Interestingly the realities of necessity were quickly embraced by most. A few brahmins and upper castes suffered as their inherited rites of purity were being made redundant.

In the nearly 74 days that the ship took to reach Fiji, a special bond grew between the 'Jehazis'. One such brotherhood developed between Ram Chander and a young man with a pock-marked face, Bhagchand. He was also a Jat and came from a village in the erstwhile Bharatpur State.

At the same time, some lifelong feuds and enmities were also born during the voyage. Somewhere along the way, Bhagchand and Ram Chander fell afoul of another group on the ship, comprising mainly of immigrants from eastern UP. This group included Isri Prasad, Moolie and Dukhia. Little did Ram Chander know how fateful these feuds were to become later in his life in Fiji!

The Surgeon Superintendent, who wielded the power on the ship, maintained a strict eye on discipline and largely succeeded in preventing any feud from turning violent on the voyage. He also enforced health requirements concerning drinking water, ventilation and sanitation and ran the hospital. A kindly gentle soul, he was deeply involved in his work, yet he was unable to prevent 15 deaths during the voyage. Besides his medical duties which included mid-voyage deliveries, he was also often called upon to name newly born babies. Some of his colleagues must have had a sense of humour all their own for one finds Indian infants born on the seas having been given names like Heavy Gale, Bhikari, Dukhee and Kangaal.

Arrival

Finally, on June 27, 1885, the "SS Ganges" sailed into Suva on the main island of Fiji, Viti Levu. Once again there was the loud din of excited chatter and a flurry of activity as the immigrants were transferred to the barges which were then towed by tugs to Nukulau Island, lying inside the Great Reef Barrier but about a kilometer off the main island. This served as the reception centre and quarantine station.

Here Ram Chander and his wife were housed in a row of barracks. The next day the Agent-General of Immigration arrived and inspections began. They were all subjected to a thorough medical check-up. Two of

Ram Chander's shipmates were rejected. One of them, a woman, died a few months later at the Suva hospital while the man was repatriated to India. Before the group left the island, ten days later, two more children had been born there.

After the quarantine the allotment process began. Some 'girmitiyas' were assigned to the Colonial Sugar Refining (CSR) Company, an Australian owned enterprise that not only owned huge plantations all over the country but also owned and ran the sugar mills till as recently as 1970 when the independent nation of Fiji bought it out. The others went to the various privately owned plantations. Ram Chander, together with 35 other men, 14 women and 3 children were allotted to Charlie Chalmers of the Penang Estate at Rakiraki on the other side of the island. All this took about ten days.

Soon Charlie Chalmer's agents in Suva arrived at Nukulau. They had brought a barge and all those allotted to Penang filed into it with their meagre worldly possessions. They then set off for their new home sailing within the reef north of Nanukuloa which was about 100 kilometers away.

On arrival at Washington Wharf, at Nanukulao, Chalmers himself was waiting at the wharf along with his Sardars to receive the new-comers. They were then marched along the cane fields to the Estate that lay several miles inland, resting at the foot of a chain of hills.

At the end of their journey the fields of sugarcane opened into a wide clearing. Rows of long barracks, the "Coolie Lines" that were to be their home for the next five years, lay before them. It was the second week of July 1885, and their long journey to their "promised land" was over.

The Sardars called for silence as they came to a halt in the clearing. Charlie Chalmers turned his horse around and began talking. He had already introduced himself and the Sardars at the wharf, and now, he was delivering his "welcome" speech. He spoke in broken 'European-Hindustani' that the newcomers had become familiar with during their increasing contacts with their European bosses. The talk was full of pious exhortations: *"Tum acha kaam karna mangta...."* (You are required to do a good job).

Eventually he finished and rode off in the direction of a gradually rising hill. The large house on top of the hill, overlooking the Estate, was his abode. At the foot of the hill lay a little cluster of smaller houses belonging to the European overseers.

After Chalmers and the others had left, Budhia, the Head Sardar, began to speak. He was a tall Rajput with a bushy upturned moustache. He pointed to the other line of barracks, whose roofs could be seen across the cane fields, and explained that these barracks housed another bunch of 33 labourers, besides himself, who had been re-engaged for another year. He then explained how they were to find their own rooms. Three single persons or a married couple with their children were allocated a room. He told them of the various facilities available, the procedures to be followed and the rules and regulations of the plantations.

Budhia also familiarised them with the procedure for the distribution of rations and informed them that five pence would be deducted from their wages every day for this. He warned them that it was illegal to sell or give away this weekly ration. After the first year, rations would be discontinued and then they could buy their own goods.

Finally, Budhia gave them a rough outline of their duties. They would be woken up at 3.30 A.M. and would have an hour to bathe, breakfast and cook their lunch. They would leave for the canefields with their Sardars who would allot the task on the fields. He also described briefly the process of task allotment. He then dispersed them, telling them to find rooms for themselves. The Sardars stayed around for a while with the labourers from the second 'Lines' who had walked over. Little groups collected as people met and talked.

Ram Chander and Padam Kaur walked over to the first structure. The Line had eight rooms on each side. They settled for the corner room at one end of the Line. The room next to theirs was occupied by fellow Jats, Ramesur, Soonkalia and their three-year-old son, Soomoria. The room on the opposite side housed Bhagchand, Narain and Bishnath Singh.

The rooms were a standard ten feet by seven feet, with a door but no windows. The inside walls stopped a few feet from the ceiling with the top part of the wooden partitions comprising a wire-netting to circulate air between the rooms to improve ventilation. The amenities included three bunks and a fire-place for cooking. The floor was mother earth. It must have been an unwelcome sight even for those who had known poverty in their home.

At 3.30 A.M. the next morning, the siren sounded at a distance and the Sardars came around to wake them up for the first day of work. An hour later, they headed for the fields. There they broke up into smaller groups, working under their own 'Sardars'. Work began early partly because the sun rises early in Fiji but more importantly because the Sardars wanted to prove to their *gora* masters that they were efficient in getting the task done by extracting maximum work by forcing the workers to reach the work site by 4.30 am. The women were in a separate gang. The overseer allocated tasks to ensure labour was done.

At the end of the allotted time the Sardars certified the work done. There was a penalty for incomplete tasks. The Sardar therefore held a life/death control over the lives of those in his charge. The sardars were "freed" labourers, i.e. they had completed their indenture and often were the worst exploiters of their countrymen.

Their treatment of women was particularly cruel; while they were paid less because they were supposed to do less work actually they were made to do as much. In addition, the Sardars made sure that wives were separated from their husbands by being given tasks in different directions away from their spouse. This was to ensure the husbands could not help their wives complete the assigned work, compelling them to seek favours from the Sardars and overseers.

Ram Chander was set to weeding and thrashing a plot of ten square "chains", broadly equal to one acre. He was a strong man and finished his task a bit before the others. For a while he helped those who had not finished. It was late afternoon when they all headed home carrying hoes on their shoulders, holding empty lunch boxes and dragging tired limbs. Back at the 'lines', they washed, cooked, ate, and sat around talking to friends for a while before turning in.

It was their religion that gave them the strength to bear the harness of their self imposed exile. Almost all plantations had their Ramayan *mandalis*. Religious festivals were celebrated with great gusto. Their culture steeped in the philosophy of surrender, fate and destiny had prepared them well for this hell which they called *narak*.

Interestingly the descendants of the Fiji girmitiyas cling to their religious and cultural heritage to this day, especially in the rural areas in Fiji, similar to what one may find deep in rural India. This heritage, sadly, is rapidly disappearing elsewhere.

This new life would involve a five-and-a-half day working week. The monotony of hard labour week after week, month after month, and year after year for five long years was the servitude to which they had agreed! But they were lucky insofar as life at the Penang Estate compared favourably with other areas in the country. It was made somewhat more tolerable by the Head Sardar, Budhia, who was a humane and a just person not commonly found amongst his breed.

On Saturday afternoons the labourers would be paid their wages. Ram Chander and Padam Kaur earned one shilling and nine pence per task. Their wages did not include rations or passage back. On holidays they would do some more work if allotted to them, otherwise they would organise wrestling bouts and 'Ramayan' reading sessions, play musical instruments and sing the 'Aalah' (Aalah was a folk song sung in praise of the two brothers Aalah and Udal the warrior rulers of Mahoba in Bundelkhand region of UP), or join in community 'Bhajans'.

Ram Chander, like most of his friends, soon acquired a taste for 'Yaqona', Fiji's national drink which remains abused by many today Yaqona, simply called grog in Fiji, is a narcotic drink made from the powdered root of the pepper plant with water.

Padam Kaur worked hard to make her tiny home hospitable. She covered the earth floor with a coating of clay mixed with cow dung, a tradition she had learnt in her own village in Jaingara. She fashioned a neat cooking place with some rocks and clay. She made her new home more habitable and somewhat respectable. The floor plastered with the clay and cow dung kept the dust and mud in control and the room relatively clean.

Thus, life progressed for the next three years. Then on April 10, 1888, a son was born to Ram Chander and Padam Kaur. The traditional Hindu religious ceremonies were performed, a priest was sent for and a feast organised. There was much rejoicing and the child was named Biri Singh. For reasons unknown, Biri got corrupted to Bere in Fiji records and that is the name he came to be known by.

Discord and More

It was an unfortunate part of plantation life that rifts would develop within this community to undermine any hope of unity and happiness. Perhaps the seeds of discord were inherent in the system of creating Sardars from amongst the labourers and giving them immense powers so that invariably factions were formed and petty intrigues took place. However, the head sardar Budhia at Penang had a calming influence.

He quelled signs of animosity and hatred and ensured that feuds were controlled. But after nearly four years of uneasy existence, even he could not control the undercurrent of resentment, rivalry and intrigue.

Ram Chander and his friends were not to escape the factional tensions of the Estate. Unfortunately, they became the centre of a particularly vicious feud the origins of which may have started on the journey to Fiji on the "Ganges". But, in truth, the roots remain shrouded in mystery and legend.

What is clear is that Ram Chander and Narain and their close friends, particularly Bhagchand and Bishnath Singh, in spite of being very popular with the majority at the Estate, had made life-long enemies of people like Isri Prasad and his friends, Moolie, Dukhia, Lalla and Dost Mohammed. Isri Prasad and his friends belonged to the same working gang and Dost Mohammed was their Sardar.

Some believe that the feud began on board the "SS Ganges" because except for Dost Mohammed all others had sailed together from Calcutta. Others talk of a quarrel involving an insult to Padam Kaur. There may be some truth in it in view of her good looks and the character of some of the people involved. This can be surmised by subsequent events and attested by court records.

The first recorded incident of the feud is a fine imposed on Lalla, in which Ram Chander, somehow, had a hand. In those days fines could be imposed on the indentured labourers for almost anything, from being 'disrespectful' to not doing their work 'properly'.

This incident and the subsequent desire for revenge must have brought the simmering feud to bubble over. The friends of Lalla conspired to take revenge on Ram Chander and his friends. To begin with, they focussed their attention on Bhagchand who was the inseparable friend of Ram Chander.

Bhagchand was set upon by five men in the dark one evening and savagely beaten up. He would have been killed had it not been for his friends arriving just in time to save him. Dukhia and Moolie were arrested for the assault.

Soon afterwards, three other men were also apprehended. They were all held in custody in the Ba gaol, close to Rakiraki town, awaiting trial at the Supreme Court in Suva.

It was amidst the tenseness of this situation that a crucial change took place that was to lead to the subversion of justice and the gaoling of two innocent men for almost three years. Budhia, the Head Sardar, was transferred to another plantation and was replaced by Dost Mohammed. Dost Mohammed, a close friend of the five men in prison, began trying to secure their release. He had just become the all-powerful Head Sardar of the Estate and did not think it would be difficult to get his wishes fulfilled.

Bhagchand being incapacitated for the time being, Dost Mohammed went to Ram Chander and ordered him to dissuade his friend Bhagchand from testifying against his assailants. Ram Chander refused to obey. Dost Mohammed then began threatening him but to no avail. The scene is vividly documented in a later appeal made by Ram Chander to the Governor of the colony.

Finally, Dost Mohammed gave up threatening Ram Chander and left with the prophetic words: "My name is Dost Mohammed. If I don't send you to prison, don't ever respect my name." "Do what you like but I will not betray my friend. And then what can you do, unless I fail to do my work?", replied Ram Chander. It was an exchange witnessed by a large number of labourers. But once it was evident that word of this heated exchange had not reached the ears of Charlie Chalmers or any other European on the Estate, Dost Mohammed began his campaign in earnest as two subsequent incidents indicate.

Soon after this exchange of words between Ram Chander and Dost Mohammed, a friend of the five men in prison claimed that a box belonging to him had been stolen. The friend of the five averred that the box had been placed in a secluded part of the road close to where Ram Chander had been working. The box was discovered but the overseer present, Mr. J. Douglas Brown, treated the matter as a joke and no one was arrested.

In the second incident, a stone with a piece of paper wrapped around it was thrown into the prison at Ba where the five men were being held. Only one person there at the time could read Hindi/Urdu and upon later enquiry, he recollected the letter as saying "Don't worry; if we cannot get you out, we will make sure that Ram Chander and his friend Bhagchand join you in prison". It was signed: "Your Friends".

The matter rested there for a while. The five men were tried in Suva. Three were given prison terms while the other two were let off with fines. But by now Dost Mohammed took to creating difficulties and making life miserable for Ram Chander and his friends at every opportunity he got. Ram Chander thought he could cope with the animosity for a few months since his period of indenture was expiring in July 1890.

But one moonlit night in June 1890, when he had just a few weeks left to serve, a fire broke out in the estate. It destroyed a small section of the sugarcane field and completely gutted the house of the Head Sardar, Dost Mohammed. Ram Chander and his wife were sleeping in their corner room when the commotion woke them up. Their friends had also got up by then and they all set off in the direction of the fire, when they were accosted by Isri Prasad and Lalla and accused of intentionally starting the fire. Soon a large crowd began to gather around the two groups in the confrontation comprising the friends of Ram Chander and others who supported Isri Prasad.

Dost Mohammed then arrived on the scene with another group of his supporters. Ram Chander and Bhagchand were separated from their friends and placed under arrest on the testimony of Lalla and Isri Prasad. The two claimed to be witnesses who had recognised from a great distance, at night, the backs of Ram Chander and Bhagchand as they were chased by a dog while fleeing from Dost Mohammed's burning house in the direction of the Lines!

A few days later, the two prisoners were taken to the Ellington wharf and put aboard the "Adi Rarongo" for the night trip to Suva. Their trial took place at the Supreme Court on 18th and 19th on July, 1890. Dost Mohammed and others came over to testify. The case against the prisoners was made even more serious by Dost Mohammed's testimony. He claimed that before setting his house on fire, the culprits had locked the door from the outside. This implied that the arson was motivated by attempted murder.

This made the case against the prisoners extremely serious. Arson was in any case amongst the most heinous crimes in a colonial society. You got 15 months for rape, but 15 years for arson. This system of priorities was typical of the colonial laws in which crime against property was always punished more severely than crime against people, especially if you were non-British.

The prisoners were found guilty of arson and sentenced to 15 years of penal servitude. Bhagchand and Ram Chander had only a few days left of their indenture period to serve out when they were arrested! Freedom from indenture was thwarted by a jail sentence.

Many questions were left unanswered at the trial. How could two men, namely Lalla and Isri Prasad, whose own house were located at a great distance from each other, be at the site of the fire at the same time? How could the supporters of the accusers recognise two figures, running away at a distance, from their backs?

No one questioned the fact that the same two men who had been the principal witnesses in another case sometime back had also been the accusers of the same two men now under trial. No one found it odd that a bright moonlit night should be chosen for the deed, or that the culprits should run straight towards the Lines thereby making sure of being apprehended by people coming from there.

Also no one took into account that if the house had been locked front outside, the only way to open it from inside would have been to break the door open. Doors in those days were locked by placing a chain through the latch outside the door and thus could not be opened from inside as Dost Mohammed had claimed to have done. Finally, the possibility of prejudiced witnesses was not taken into account at all. These questions should have been asked during the trial by the government pleader but amazingly nobody raised them.

III

CHAPTER

The Epic Struggle: Padam Kaur's Fight for Justice

"Dum Spiro Spero: As long as I breathe, I hope for everything"

Leon Trotsky

Dost Mohammed and his friends returned to Rakiraki, after the trial, triumphant at having redeemed their pledge to send Bhagchand and Ram Chander to prison. On their way home they anchored on a beach off the Ellington Wharf. So despised were they by the workers on the Estate that here they were set upon by two Fijians and two Indians who worked on the plantation adjoining the beach. The attackers were close friends of the overseer of the plantation, Bernard and Budhia who was the head Sardar.

Dost Mohammed and his friends managed to escape and filed a case against their four assailants. The case was heard by Mr. Joske, the Stipendiary Magistrate at Ba. Magistrate Joske dismissed the case for lack of evidence, though he noted on the file that he had no doubt that Bernard and Budhia were involved in the attack on the complainants.

Since Dost Mohammed could not get his revenge on Bernard and Budhia, he now directed his ire at Ram Chander's wife, Padam Kaur and her cousin, Narain. In any case, the workers had anticipated that now that Ram Chander and Bhagchand were not around, Dost Mohammed would target his vengeance on Padam Kaur and Narain.

Thus a group of old friends organised to protect them against any mischief. The majority of other workers at the plantation, who had previously remained neutral, recognising the monstrous injustice, also became sympathetic to Padam Kaur and Narain. They kept a close eye to ensure that Padam Kaur was constantly protected. In addition they helped her complete the unfairly large task allotted to her each day by Dost Mohammed.

Frustrated and unable to get at Padam Kaur, the Sardar turned his attention to Narain. One day Narain was accused of stealing a box. This was a trumped up charge as had happened with Ram Chander earlier. The charge could not be sustained due to complete lack of evidence. Additionally, the other workers at the plantation vociferously defended Narain.

Such defiance of a head Sardar was possible now because most of the ex-"Ganges" labourers had finished their indenture and were preparing to leave. A new lot of labourers from India had come on board the "Allanshaw" on the 17th of May 1890. They would be replacing those who wanted to leave, and those leaving would no longer be at the mercy of Dost Mohammed.

At this stage, a rumour swept through the plantation that Padam Kaur's safety was at risk. Her friends had learnt that a conspiracy was being hatched against her. Padam Kaur had already decided that she would go to Suva once her indenture period had been completed so that she could be closer to her husband who was incarcerated in the prison there.

For her safety her friends advised that she should leave for Suva immediately on completing her *girmit* contract. The exact date of departure needed to be kept a secret as Dost Mohammed's vengeance posed a major threat both to her and to her infant son. Her plantation friends were also concerned that she would be defenceless once she left their protection.

Often under an oppressive Sardar, a counter group would form around someone else. This leader need not be a defiant rebel. It sufficed if he was respected by a majority of the workers. After the departure of Ram Chander, this position had been filled by Badri Maharaj, a young 20 year-old Garhwali who had just arrived in the "Allanshaw".

Badri Maharaj was a rare person. He was literate, physically very strong and of kind disposition. These qualities made him a natural leader. These qualities would some years later lead him to become the first Indian Member of the Legislative Council. Almost a century later, Ram Chander's grandson Bhagwan Singh and Badri Maharaj's son would form a very close relationship. This friendship would continue into several subsequent generations. Perhaps the following paragraphs will shed light on the sustaining of this beautiful relationship.

Within two months of being at the plantation and uninvolved in the long feud which now threatened Padam Kaur's safety, Badri Maharaj organised her escape with the backing of the local Fijian chief Ratu Jone Madraiwiwi. Legend has it that one night, Badri and five hefty Fijian workers left the plantation with Padam Kaur and her two-year-old son, Bere Singh. The Fijians belonged to the local villages and knew all the walking trails from the Penang plantation to the Nanukuloa wharf. They hurried through the night, avoiding the main road and using side tracks through the cane fields, They made it just in time to get Padam Kaur on to the boat "Adi Rarongo" which was leaving for Suva.

The next day Padam Kaur arrived at Suva. With her she had a letter which had been drafted by Badri Maharaj, and signed by almost all Indians at Penang Estate vouching for Ram Chander's innocence and alleging that the charges which led to his imprisonment were baseless. Padam Kaur would go to a Roman Catholic missionary, Brother M Columba in Suva. He was sympathetic to the plight of Indian indentured labourers and had started one of the first schools for their children. Columba received her kindly, listened to her story, gave her food and shelter and promised her assistance in her quest for justice. The compassion shown convinced Padam Kaur to be converted to Christianity. She now had a new name — 'Parbotti'.

Even as Parbotti was knocking on countless doors seeking her husband's release, Ram Chander had begun his own battle for justice from inside Suva Gaol. His first volley was a long petition written by him in his own handwriting in September 1890. It was written on both sides of a sheet of paper.

After 85 years, when discovered in the Fiji National Archives, due to Suva's humid climate, the ink had seeped through the sides making some parts of it illegible. The author of the letter was obviously literate and the language used was a combination of Urdu and a particular dialect of Hindi spoken around Agra, the *Braj Bhasa*. The epistle was sorrowful but states his case with eloquence. At the top of every page was the annotation: "Shri Ramji Sada Sahai" (Lord Ram is forever with us).

Ram Chander's letter was sent to the Agent-General of Immigration for translation. This eloquent cry for justice suffered a poor translation and ended up sounding like a pathetic plea. The letter is in fact the humble pleadings of a dignified man who is bewildered by the injustice which has deprived him of his freedom and life. In the portion that was visible, the letter read:

> "Sir,
>
> With folded hands and in great helplessness and wretchedness, I offer my salutations to you....I am in great tribulation that in the Queen's Raj a plot should have obtained me such punishment....I cannot conceive up to this moment how falsehood could have prevailed over me...."

The translated letter of Ram Chander was sent to the Attorney–General, who was responsible to advise the Governor on prosecutions and reopening of the cases for retrial if there was new evidence available. However, the Attorney-General saw no reason why the Governor should interpose in the matter. In his opinion, the trial had been fair and there was no new evidence. He saw no substance in the pleadings of the petitioner and noted that he fully agreed with the sentence.

In the meantime, Padam Kaur, now known as Parbotti, moved around Suva pleading her husband's case. She was resourceful, showed courage and determination in spite of the many disappointments and dashed hopes.

Parbotti faced a devastating blow when she found that one of her and her husband Ram Chander's *jehazi* mate, Ramdin, had cheated her of the then huge sum of £7 from the money entrusted to him for her husband's legal fees. The amount represented approximately six months' wages for both Ram Chander and Padam Kaur. Among the indentured Indian community *jehazis* were considered brothers and sisters; they formed the new family structure to replace the lost loved ones at home in India. Ramdin's perfidy in defrauding a vulnerable woman, a *jehazi behen* (sister) was unforgivable among those who declared themselves *jehazi* kin.

But there were other moments of hope and support from other friends and even perfect strangers. It was a measure of Parbotti's demeanour and the compelling nature of her story that she invariably moved her interlocutors. The many unanswered questions about the case and discrepancies in the evidence clearly pointed to a miscarriage of justice. The most pertinent of these issues was the well known enmity between Ram Chander and Bhagchand and the so-called witnesses to the crime. Over the next two and a half years, Parbotti persisted in pleading her husband's case to a host of people, officers of the Colonial administration, lawyers and well meaning individuals, who could help in her quest to get her husband released.

One English officer, who Parbotti had met only once, went out of his way to help her. This was H. J. Milne, Superintendent of the multi-purpose and multifunctional Depot for Immigrants, who also tried to find her a job there. As he said in a note he wrote to the Governor. "...I have seen this woman who is staying by my order, temporarily at the Depot. She appears to be a superior sort of woman, apparently very respectable. I am sorry for her present helpless condition. She has a young child and..."

Sometime later, Parbotti managed to engage another solicitor, Mr. C.H. Irvine, to write a formal petition to the Governor on behalf of the two prisoners. The solicitor had reservations about the new petition since no new evidence had come forth. However, this reluctance was quickly put aside when Padam Kaur defied convention and paid him in advance.

The formal petition drawn by Mr. Irvine reached the Governor who ordered an enquiry. Unfortunately, the Magistrate who was entrusted with the enquiry utilised the services of Dost Mohammed as an interpreter! For obvious reasons, nothing new came out of the inquiry and the Magistrate's report recommended that the petition be rejected.

This must have been a shattering blow but Parbotti refused to give up hope. Her persistence is vouched for in a series of notes on several files dated around that period from senior officials of the colonial administration. The notings testify to the persistence, courage and faith of a woman refusing to admit defeat and carrying on the lonely struggle for justice and her husband's liberty.

In a typical note of this kind, on a file addressed to the Colonial Secretary, who functioned as Chief Secretary to the Governor, an official writes, ".. the wife of one of the prisoners has been continually urging me to try and get her husband out, asserting his innocence". He goes on to say how the evidence, as he sees it, points to a false charge with the witnesses manufacturing evidence to get a conviction.

Finally, Parbotti went back to her original solicitor, Mr. J.H. Garrick, who had helped her frame two previous petitions in Ram Chander's name, which had been rejected even though Garrick was a solicitor with substantial heft. He was a prominent solicitor and Notary Public who was licenced to practice in the Supreme Courts of Fiji, Victoria, New South Wales and Queensland in Australia, and in New Zealand. He was also a very busy man. He advised Parbotti to try again, this time petitioning in her own name.

The document, signed by J. H. Garrick on 7 October 1890, was written in the usual petition style and was addressed to the Governor, Sir John Bates Thurston. In it, wrote Garrick in the style of those times, "Your petitioner humbly sheweth" six points for the Governor's consideration. Apart from the known inconsistencies, the petition drew attention to Dost Mohammed's role as the interpreter in the previous enquiry.

Fortunately, this time there was some new evidence too. A free Indian, named Manohar, residing in Suva at that time, was willing to swear that Dost Mohammed, who was then in Suva prior to his departure for India, had told him Manohar that "Your petitioner's" husband had not committed the arson but he Dost Mohammed knew who had done so.

In the covering letter, J. H. Garrick wrote to the Governor:

> "I have prepared this petition and am forwarding it not in a professional capacity but from a conviction of the innocence of the prisoner of the crime he was convicted of. I have had considerable experience of the principal witness for the Crown and believe him (referring to Dost Mohammad) unworthy of credit. During twenty years' experience of the Bar, I have not known a conviction obtained that I believe so strongly condemned an innocent man."

The Governor received the petition and forwarded it to the Colonial Secretary with a note mentioning the dubious aspects of the case and concluded: "...my mind is seriously disturbed with the propriety of the verdict and the sentence on the petitioner's husband which consequently followed... Let the Superintendent of Police make the most careful enquiries and give a report with as little delay as can be."

The Superintendent passed on the file to A.D. Joske, the Stipendiary Magistrate at Ba, the same official who had carried out the enquiries after Solicitor Irvine's petition. That petition was in Ram Chander's name in which his testimony had been recorded in *Brij Bhasha*. Joske had then made the tragic error of engaging Dost Mohammed to translate from the *Braj Bhasha*.

This time Joske carried out a more extensive enquiry. He visited Penang and carried out many interviews including that of Coster, the Assistant Manager, Birja, the new Head Sardar, and numerous workers on the estate. In his report, Joske reversed his own previous defence of Dost Mohammad's character and contended that the "public Indian opinion at the Estate was that it had been a trumped-up charge."

He concluded by saying that although in such cases it was nearly impossible to pin down anything positive, particularly at such a late stage, he strongly recommended clemency. He pointed out that if the prisoners were guilty then they had suffered enough, but if they were innocent then "the prospects before them were truly appalling.

The file once again returned to the Colonial Secretary's desk in Suva. He "respectfully submitted" it to the Governor with a note saying: "Nothing conclusive but all pointing in one direction."

On the 3rd of May 1893, the Governor replied to the Colonial Secretary. He wrote:

> "I have decided to exercise the prerogative of pardon in this case and to remit the remainder of the sentence imposed upon the convicts. Please direct the Superintendent of Police to convey the pardon of Her Majesty to the Prisoners and discharge them forthwith."

Ram Chander and Bhagchand stepped out of Suva gaol on May 18, 1894, having spent two years and ten months there. It had taken almost three years for the wheels of justice to turn the complete circle.

Fiji was fortunate in having a number of just and fair men at the helm of its colonial administration. Men like A.R. Coates, the Inspector of Indian Immigration, Frederick Sabben, the Superintendent of the Suva Gaol, H.J. Milne, the Superintendent of the Imigration Depot and the Governor himself. They had all gone out of their way to ensure justice was done.

Ram Chander was provided employment at the Depot on the then bountiful salary of £24 per year, with rations and quarters. Parbotti was also given a job with the Government. Later Ram Chander was promoted and made warder at the Prison Hospital in addition to his job at the Depot. The Fiji Blue Book that lists all government appointments lists Parbotti as Female Warder at Suva Gaol from 1st January 1898 to 1901 at an annual salary of £12.

Despite this new success, the period of happiness, however, could not erase the pain and suffering which lingered in their memories. Ram Chander and Parbotti could have made a comfortable life in Fiji but they eventually decided to return home to India. On the 8th of July 1901, after spending 16 years in Fiji, Ram Chander, Parbotti and their 13 year-old son, Bere Singh, returned to India on board the "Fazilka-II".

IV

CHAPTER

My Grandfather, Bere Singh in Fiji

When Ram Chander and Padam Kaur, who had also adopted the name Parbotti on her conversion to Christianity, left the shores of Fiji aboard the "Fazilka-II" on July 8, 1901, little did they realise that within a decade their only child Bere Singh would return to those very shores in search of his future. Bere was born to Ram Chander and Padam Kaur, we may recall, on April 10, 1888, almost three years after they had come to Fiji.

Having seen the Suva Gaol and visited what was once the first shelter for Indian widows and single mothers, I can only imagine the early days of my grandfather Bere Singh's life. There was little security, shelter or fixed meals. He would have clung to his mother, as she knocked on many doors in her epic fight against the immense injustice done to his father. He would have carried memories of his mother's desperate struggle for justice. But as with any growing child his sense of adventure would have been kindled in this small and beautiful town with its lush vegetation and he would have climbed many a mango and guava trees to pick and eat the fruits.

However, the last three years of his life in Fiji, when his parents were still there, must have been the happiest ones. Both parents were employed by the Government and they lived in Government quarters at the Suva Gaol. Ironically, the Suva Gaol had been not only his home but prior to that it had been the one regular place he and his mother used to visit. These visits must have been keenly anticipated by the child. He would meet his father who lived in that imposing building surrounded by huge walls. But perhaps the most vivid in his memory would be of his mother's sense of dignity and self-respect. Even amongst the most challenging conditions she provided her with warmth and security. Bere Singh's own personality would have been deeply influenced. Later events would bear testimony to this.

Bere Singh was one of the first Indian children to be enrolled into a new school that had just been started by the Marist Brothers. This religious order was started in France and the Roman Catholic bishop in Fiji had invited the brothers to help him minister to the downtrodden, mostly families and children of the girmityas. Towards the end of the 19th Century, a primary school was established to provide education for Indian children. The Marist Brothers exemplified the Christian Missionary spirit which has transformed many communities.

Marist Brothers' School grew into one of the most prestigious and effective educational institutions in Fiji. Several generations of the nation's leadership in politics, the professions and society have been groomed in this school. Its alumni includes the first prime minister of independent Fiji, Ratu Sir Kamisese Mara, the current Prime Minister, Frank Bainimarama, and scores of doctors, lawyers, surveyors, and educators. Thus Bere Singh would have received a sound early education with a balance of secular skills grounded strongly in Christian teachings of compassion for the less fortunate.

Once they returned to India, to their native village on the banks of the river Khari near Agra, Bere Singh was despatched by his parents to the historic Jat House in Agra for his further schooling. Jat House was a community facility for children coming from rural areas to study in Agra. He shared a room with a quiet and studious colleague with whom he developed a close lifelong relationship. This young man would later play a crucial role in pre-partition Punjab's political life, particularly in undivided Punjab. His name was Chhotu Ram who later changed the course of my father's life.

Even as he studied in Agra, Bere Singh continued to be in touch with his former teacher, Brother M. Columba of the Marist Brothers' School in Suva. Brother Columba was to later settle down in the nickel-rich New

Caledonia, a French territory in the Pacific. From there he would write moving letters to his former pupil consistently reinforcing two things. Firstly, that Jesus Christ was the only true God who will always love him and secondly, to disregard his father's advice and return to Fiji to seek his future there.

Bere Singh's conversion to Christianity, which likely happened along with his mother's, was because the Christian missionaries practiced what they preached. They cared for the oppressed, the downtrodden and those who suffered. Many Indians converted in those early days for this reason even though they also had more pragmatic reasons such as education and employment. While many lived their new faith, some were outwardly Christians but in their hearts retained their traditional religion whether it was Islam or Hinduism. Bere Singh was one of those. When he finally returned to his village, his devotion to his Hindu roots re-emerged.

My father, Bhagwan Singh, in his autobiographical book, "Fiji: My Father's Land", wrote about his early fascination with a far away country called Fiji. He wrote about watching the *dakiya*, the village postman, gingerly crossing the rickety wooden bridge over the river Khari. He would come from the neighbouring Basaiya village faithfully once a month to regularly deliver an envelope with colourful stamps to his father. Bere Singh would read the letters and then would carefully hide them in his steel trunk.

My father told me he would climb the big peepal tree in the open space outside the house to hide from his father. There, he would read the occasional letter, which he was able to secrete, written in Hindi from his father's friends. But till he learnt English, in his early teens, there was the one regular letter he could not decipher. His natural curiosity was further fanned by the fact that on the very next day his father would dress up and leave for Agra. Later he realised that the letter contained his pension. He needed to go to Agra to the bank as banks were not located in rural districts.

Ironically, even as Bere Singh's parents were opposed to his even thinking of going back to Fiji, years later Bere Singh would be just as paranoid in his objection to the thought of his own son ever going to Fiji even for a visit.

Back in his native village from Fiji, Bere Singh completed his matriculation at the Agra Collegiate School where he seemed to have been an average student, earning "Conduct Good" remarks from his Headmaster. In early 1909 he progressed to St. John's Collegiate School, Agra for higher studies but family circumstances compelled him to leave academics to start earning his livelihood.

Why he left his studies abruptly is alluded to in his application for employment addressed to the Magistrate, Police Force, Suva (Fiji) where he says:

> "The reason for my dictating all this is that my father has run into debt over head and ears owing to the recent famine and now he wants me to enter service so that I may supply him with money. I, therefore, request you and beseech you to take me in your service for on account of the above mentioned fact, I have to cut short my student career which is a great shock and sorrow to me. Hence I hope that you will have pity on me and will appoint me interpreter in your Court. If not that I further hope that you will be kind enough to procure me a post elsewhere..."

It seems as if the cycle of events had come to a full circle. A generation ago, many of the first Indians to set sail to Fiji were those who had been impoverished by famine. Many others needed to repay their debts, having been driven away from their farms by greedy landlords. Although Ram Chander had chosen to go to Fiji to avoid a family dispute, almost three decades later, his own son was preparing to sail to Fiji because of famine related impoverishment. According to the Agra Gazette of that time, a particularly devastating drought had ravaged the region.

Bere Singh wrote similar letters to each and every friend and employer of his father. It is a measure of the respect won by his parents during their stay in Fiji that most replied despite the challenges of postal communication between Fiji and India at that time.

A crumbling one-page letter dated the 26th June 1909 which Bere Singh received from Fiji said:

> "I had spoken to Mr. Gwan, the Inspector-General of Prisons, and asked him to write to you regarding employment at this gaol. I trust he may be able to fall in with your wishes so that you may be able to help your deserving but unfortunate parents...."

This letter was signed by Frederick Sabben, the man who had been his father's jailor, employer, benefactor and friend.

As the only child of his parents, Bere Singh was under tremendous pressure to find employment so that he could rid his parents of their debt and support them in their old age. In his search for employment he was supported by members of the colonial bureaucracy and Christian friends, both in Fiji and in and around Agra, as also by his academic mentors.

Towards the end of 1909, Bere Singh received several offers of employment form Fiji and started collecting funds for his fare thus pushing his parents further into debt. He soon set sail for those distant islands where he was born.

On March 14, 1910, some eight years and seven months after he had first sailed out of Suva harbour along with his parents, Bere Singh wrote a formal letter from Nukulau depot, to the Agent-General of Immigration. He requested him to:

> "...Kindly find me an employment as a Clerk or Interpreter in any office because the Head Constableship is not the sort where I can improve my education and besides, I think myself better qualified to do the work above mentioned...."

Coming across this letter 65 years later at the Fiji Archives, I, Bere Singh's grandson would be mildly surprised to read the next paragraph:

> "...As regards my qualifications, I am a convert Christian by religion. I am educated up to the Matriculation Class and passed my Middle School examination in 1908 both in Hindi and English."

The letter is signed: "J.T. Bere Singh". This was the first and last mention of his conversion to Christianity that I am aware of.

Family legends had spoken of Bere Singh's mother's conversion to Christianity during her epic battle to secure her husband' freedom two decades ago. According to one of the numerous letters that Brother Columba, his former teacher at Marist Brothers in Suva wrote to Bere Singh, the initials "J. T." probably stood for Joseph Thomas.

Bere Singh's civil service record as shown in the Blue Book of the Fiji Civil Service shows that he joined as Assistant Clerk to Pay & Quartermaster, Fiji Constabulary on March 21, 1910. Within nine weeks he was promoted to the post of Clerk, Prisons Department.

There is on record a very interesting representation made by Bere Singh within weeks of his arrival in Fiji. The pride and sense of self-respect imbibed from his parents would make Bere Singh again and again struggle for his beliefs and values. It would keep him in the Government's eyes and often get him into a lot of trouble as would be evident from his subsequent representations to senior government authorities later.

In this petition dated April 6, 1910, addressed to the Agent-General of Immigration, Bere Singh states:

"Sir,

With due respect and humble submission, I beg leave to draw your kind attention to the following:

That I, your humble servant, worked on the SS "Songola" on the same level with a compounder named U. Joseph.

Baboo Maitra, who was assistant to the Surgeon Supdt., was in charge of the dispensary and hospitals, and another Madrassi Baboo Sammy to assist him in treating patients and preparing remedies. B. Zahar Alla's duty was to attend to the cooking of both Madras and Calcutta (means cooking both South Indian and North Indian food) and inspect things and report cases to the Superintendent.

Joseph and myself were in charge of all the sanitation and cleanliness of the ship and to call the roll and inspect the feeding. The time-table which I herewith attach. None of the *Madrassi* Baboos could speak Hindustani, neither could the Calcutta (Baboos) speak *Tamil or Telugu,* therefore, Joseph was to oversee all the *Madrassis'* work only, and I the Calcutta's!

By mentioning these facts, I do mean to claim the rights of the junior assistant (Joseph) but not totally because I did all the work similar to what he did and worked more days for which the Surgeon Superintendent is extremely pleased and knows that I deserve a good gratuity. A Certificate given by him I herewith enclose for your honour to testify as to how I carried out my duties at sea.

Baboo Joseph for his reward got £23 (+ six pence per head =£26.13.6), and a free passage back to India as a second class passenger. I only respectfully beg leave to request the Government to be kind enough to grant the request which I humbly make.

All the Indians coming from India to serve in Fiji Government receive a good pay and a free return passage in coming and going back to India. Why should I be deprived of the same when beside paying my own fare I worked day and night on the Emigrant vessel, and my father and mother had been loyal and faithful servants to the Fiji Government for a good many years, working at the Korovou Jail, and I have offered myself to do the same and will try my best to give every satisfaction.

I most humbly request your honour to give a favourable consideration.

For this act of kindness, I shall be much indebted and thankful

I am, Sir
Your Most Obedient Servant,
J.T. BERE SINGH"

Bere Singh received a reply dated July 4, 1910 from the Inspector-General of Constabulary to the effect that:

> "His Excellency the Governor has been pleased to direct that in recognition of services rendered as Assistant to the compounders on board SS "Sangola" from India to Fiji, the cost of your passage be limited (meaning one way fare reimbursement only) and you will not receive any further remuneration in respect of these services."

However, these were mere trivial skirmishes compared to a major confrontation which would, even decades later, be told and retold with pride by old-timers in Fiji. In it, racial prejudice and colonial clumsiness were challenged by an educated Indian. As in his father's case, Bere Singh found that his willingness to stand up and fight, combined with the famous British sense of 'fair play', led to a victory of sorts.

In an astounding and unheard-of step, Bere Singh wrote an official representation to his immediate boss, the Stipendiary Magistrate in Nadi, seeking the Government's help in taking legal action against a European gentleman by the name of Mr. Britten for having misbehaved with him in public.

In this representation, dated the 9th September 1912, he stated:

> "Sir,
>
> I most regretfully beg to bring to your kind notice that on last Saturday evening about 6 P.M., I was standing near Averan Singh's tent at Waqadra when I heard Mr. Britten calling me at a chain (10/12 feet distance) away. I ran over to him. He gave orders, "Tum ghora pakro" (you hold the horse). I asked, "What do you take me for, Mr. Britten?" Indignantly, he repeated again his command, "Tum ghora pakro". I answered: "I won't do it: get someone else." In the meantime, as there was a big crowd, an Indian came forward and took hold of the horse.
>
> He got out of the strap cursing me and went to turn out a few Europeans who were in his dray behind and came back to me saying in an authoritative tone: "Look here, whenever I tell you to hold my horse you will have to do it." "Not I", I re-joined, "and ta'pence do I care for who you are." On which, he drove away saying nothing further.

From the exact words passed given above, you will learn how maliciously I was insulted to be degraded in the eyes of such a vast crowd of people there. Luckily the Indian got hold of the horse otherwise my fate would probably have been the whip.

With an object to obtain satisfaction from my insulter, I approach you requesting that you will be good enough to bring this grievance of mine before the notice of the Hon. Colonial Secretary as this is not the only instance where an Indian employee of the government has been insulted, assaulted and ill-treated by the Company's men.

They are not educated men and they know nothing of India or its immemorial traditions; consequently confuse all the Indians here in the same condemnation, while an Indian of good family who in the opinion of all cultivated people take a very high place in human family, are classed and treated all alike by them. On reference Mr. S.B. Scott-Young, Inspector of Constabulary, Nadi, Lautoka will be able to furnish many instances of this sort against others and Britten as well. Not been punished, they have taken an upper hand on us.

I therefore, implore that the Government will consider my grievance and innocence in the matter and will give him a lesson which he will bear in mind not to interfere with whom he has nothing whatsoever to do. If this request cannot be entertained, may it please the Government to help me in taking a legal action against him.

For this act of sympathy, I shall be ever thankful.

I am, Sir,
Your Obedient Servant
BERE SINGH"

The word that he had been rudely spoken to and that he had given a fitting reply spread like wildfire among the Fiji Indians. Bere Singh was still in his early 20s but soon became a widely respected man, symbolising as he did the search of the Indian community for their identity and to preserve their dignity.

Interestingly enough, even in that remote outpost of the colonial empire, there were enough colonial masters who saw the fairness of Bere Singh's appeal. In my hours spent in the Fiji National Archives in 1973, the documents that recorded evidence of this sentiment held particular interest for me.

Following Bere Singh's written complaint, the colonial bureaucracy moved into action and an Office file with number 5777/1912 was opened in the Colonial Secretary's office on the subject. The first notation dated

12th September 1912, addressed to the Hon' Colonial Secretary, pointed out that:

> "Bere Singh, Clerk/Interpreter to Nadi Court, asks for permission to prosecute Mr. Britten under the Summary Convictions Ordinance for insulting language." *Under the provisions of this ordinance a person if proven guilty could be penalised and a fine may be imposed on him in the first hearing itself. If a person is found guilty of repeating the same offence for two three times he could be both penalised and imprisoned*
>
> The Colonial Secretary's office, while underlining the words "asks for permission", noted in the margin against the above note: "This is not accurate. See Bere Singh's letter," and made a further query: "Have there not been similar complaints against this employee of the C.S.R. Company – Mr. Britten?"

The Colonial Secretary received a typical bureaucratic reply:

> "I am not aware that similar complaints have been made against Mr. Britten, who is the C.S.R.Coy's Cane Inspector at Nadi, I think. He is without any record in this office. The expression "Ghora pakar" means only 'hold the horse'; the offence is in Bir (Bere) Singh's eyes that he should be told to do this before other Indians, I gather.
>
> Overseers and planters generally are inclined to regard Interpreters and Constables who associate with indentured immigrants as intriguers, and look upon them with suspicion. If Bere Singh's account is correct, Mr. Britten may have acted with intention.
>
> I attach papers relating to the complaint of Kanagasa Bhai, who is, I think, also Interpreter at Nadi".

However, there was someone who was not quite keen to take up the case of a wronged Indian Government employee because the above notation is followed by this:

> "Submitted the Magistrate at Nadi be requested to inform the interpreter that the Government is unable to take any proceedings on his behalf and that he is at liberty to take such action in the matter as he may elect or be advised to take.
>
> A word of explanation may help. The exchange between the Colonial Secretary and the other unnamed official represents two divergent viewpoints often found among the colonial bureaucracy. One section, represented here by the Colonial Secretary, wanted the law to be implemented without consideration of master and subject. Hence, his query about other similar complaints against Mr. Britten. His minion notes that there is no such record found, leaving open the tantalising possibility that a more diligent search

> may come up with a different outcome. In keeping with his non-empathetic approach he goes on to suggest that Bere Singh should be advised that the administration would not pursue his complaint but he is free to do so of his own will and, more important, at his own cost.
>
> But the colonial Secretary was obviously a more farsighted man. His reply was unambiguous: "I think you should invite Mr…'s attention to this matter and send him a copy of the enclosed letter. If Mr. Britten did speak to the writer as stated, the latter has good grounds for complaint. Our Indian Officers are entitled to protection."

The Colonial Secretary's remarks brought forth prompt action. Mr. Britten was asked for his version, which was submitted to the Colonial Secretary. But, in another display of his dilatory attitude, the official quoted earlier also appended the specious suggestion that a response be sought from Mr. Britten's boss, the manager of the CSR Company, on Mr. Britten's reply; the justification being that the manager's view would represent his understanding of Mr. Britten's normal conduct with the Indian origin staff. The real objective, of course, was to delay the process of justice and test Bere Singh's resolve.

However, the Colonial Secretary was once again explicit in his response: "Has the Stipendiary Magistrate any remarks to make? I take grave exception to Mr. Britten calling a Government official a "low caste Indian."

The Acting Stipendiary Magistrate, Nadi's response to the Colonial Secretary also speaks for itself. He wrote:

> "If anything could serve to support the genuineness of Bere Singh's grievance, it would be the tone of Mr. Britten's explanation.
>
> To class a man of Bere Singh's type as a 'low caste Indian, is insolence pure and simple.
>
> Even rank ignorance would hardly mitigate the offence of such an opprobrious epithet, and I do not think that such a plea can be sent up on behalf of Mr. Britten."
>
> Sd/
> S. M. Nadi
> 31-12-1912
>
> PS: "I may mention that Mr. Britten is out of the Colony at present on six months leave.
>
> Sd/-
> S.M. Nadi

It is easy to interpret what had happened. Once it was clear that the Colonial Secretary and the Stipendiary Magistrate were intent on following on Bere Singh's complaint and the likelihood was that Mr. Britten could well be publicly chastised, it was thought prudent to send him away from Fiji on six months' leave.

The incident had a salutary effect on the Fiji Indians. The early civil servants of Indian origin in Fiji were emboldened in their fight against racial prejudice. Bere Singh's stand earned him the respect and affection not only of the Indian community but also of the more far sighted section of the colonial bureaucracy. For the remaining decade that Bere Singh was in Fiji, this stand of his often placed him in the forefront of similar attempts to fight for the Fiji Indians' self-respect.

This incident was one of the early blows struck by literate Indian opinion against the inequities of the colonial system in Fiji and it came at a time when increasingly powerful opinion was building up in India against emigration as a whole.

The decade starting in 1910 saw a series of mutually-reinforcing actions by several historically famous figures coalesce to deliver a body blow to the whole process of emigration. By this time Mohandas Karamchand Gandhi had already spent many years fighting for the rights of Indians in South Africa, where indentured labour had mainly settled in Natal. Much has been written about his early years fighting the mighty British Empire for the right to self-respect of the Indians in South Africa. The truth is that his later battles are the ones that have remained in the public mind and earned him the title of 'Mahatma'. That this frail old man based his first political battle against the enslavement of Indians overseas is seldom remembered.

Inspired by Gandhi's battles in South Africa, which had been closely followed by the Indian elite, and riding on the contemporary upsurge of Indian nationalism. Gopal Krishna Gokhale moved a resolution in the Imperial Legislative Council in London, demanding that the ILS be abolished not only in Natal but throughout the world. In 1910, when Bere Singh was sailing to Fiji, legislation was passed by the Imperial Legislative Council giving wide-ranging powers to the Government of India to prohibit emigration to any country.

Yet another great blow to the system was struck by Tota Ram Sanadhya's book published in 1914: *"Fiji Dweep Men Mere Ikkis Varsh"* (My Twenty one Years in Fiji Islands), a copy of which I read as a child by purloining it from my father's papers.

Tota Ram Sanadhya is a legendary figure about whom songs are sung in Fiji even today. Born in Firozabad, near Agra (Agra again !!!!) Tota Ram came from a poor Brahmin family and was recruited as an indentured labour for Fiji under false pretences in 1893, then barely 16. He had a harrowing five years as a plantation labour but after his tenure finished, he chose to stay back in Fiji to help the girmitiyas, even educating himself to become a priest and sing religious songs to rally and uplift the Indians. He returned to India in 1913 and published his famous book the year after which created a furore and even led to an invitation to Sanadhya to address the meeting of the Indian National Congress in Madras in 1915, the year Gandhi returned to India.

Before writing his own book Sanadhya had been a major influence behind a book published in 1910, "Fiji of Today", which was one of the most brutally explicit descriptions of the lives of the indentured labourers to have appeared till then. Published in London, the book had been written by an Australian Methodist Missionary, Reverend J. W. Burton, who had spent almost 10 years working with Indians in the Rewa district of Fiji, an experience which made him into a committed foe of the indenture system. The book caused a sensation in Fiji also where the British had deliberately kept the two ethnic communities, the native Fijians and the Indentured Indian workers, so segregated that the local people were not aware what was happening with the Indians on the plantations.

Public opinion was forcing authorities in India, in Britain and in Fiji to re-evaluate this barbarous system. The critics of the system pursued it relentlessly. Gokhale moved a resolution in the Imperial Legislative Council again in 1912 for the total abolition of the system. In one of his most famous speeches, Gokhale analysed the system in detail and concluded that "it was based on fraud and maintained by force; that the safeguards were illusory; that it was accompanied by frightful reality and that it was degrading to the people of India". This motion was unanimously supported by the Indian Members of the Council.

The momentum against the system was beginning to snowball when the First World War intervened. Labour was now required for the war effort. However, the slow wheels of history had begun their inexorable motion and change in attitudes continued. This can best be seen from a circular sent to all the District Commissioners in Fiji in 1915 ordering them to refrain from using the derogatory word "coolie" and to replace it with "indentured Indian immigrant".

Another historical figure who played a key role in this issue was Reverend CF Andrews, Gandhi's close associate, who made two visits to Fiji in that critical decade. His second visit had the unofficial sanction of the then Viceroy, Lord Hardinge. Andrews was accompanied on this trip by Reverend W.M. Pearson, a lecturer at Delhi's St Stephen's College, which was my own alma mater. By the time their report was published in 1916, and perhaps because of it, Lord Hardinge, an admirer of Andrews, was able to announce that he had secured the promise of the British Government for the abolition of the system "in due course". Andrews was grateful on the announcement and wrote:

> "We feel today that God has overwhelmed us with His goodness in allowing us to have our share in this great fact. It means the taking away of one more abomination from God's earth."

However, the plantation lobby in Fiji, led by the largest company, CSR, continued to fight an effective rear-guard battle against the abolition. The argument was now switched in favour of less crude forms of assisted immigration to the colonies. Historians feel that Andrews might have accepted this but for the firm intervention of Mahatma Gandhi who persuaded Andrews that any other system would inevitably re-introduce the same malady. There were others, in India, as well as abroad, who felt a complete prohibition of emigration would deprive lakhs of Indians the right to better their prospects away from home.

In 1917, Rev. Andrews went to Fiji yet again. His reports from Fiji this time were more devastating. It was on this journey through the village of Fiji that he earned his lifelong title "Deenbandhu", friend of the poor. This time Andrews found a basic but crucial difference in the Indian community: a growing awareness about themselves had been creeping in and taking roots. The one single factor symbolising this was their growing eagerness for education, not only for themselves but primarily for their children.

In one of his earlier visits, Rev. Andrews had started an elementary primary school in a bure (a kind of hut made on a square platform on four wooden pillars and covered with a thatched cover made of straw) inside an Indian village. He specifically encouraged the small children of girmitiyas to walk long distances to attend school. Due to Rev. Andrews' persuasive powers families volunteered from both communities, native Fijians and Fiji Indians, to send their children to schools set up by Indians.

One such school was the Wairuku Indian School set up in 1898 by Pandit Badri Maharaj, a farmer and indentured labour who had come to Fiji in 1889. It was in this school, at which Rev. CF Andrews also taught, that a life long friendship was formed between Lala Sukuna and Badri Maharaj's eldest son, Raghavanand.

(Ratu Sir Lala Sukuna, as he later came to be known, is considered the father of the modern state of Fiji. He was the son of a high chief of Fiji. Ratu Sukuna later went for collegiate education to New Zealand and went to Oxford University to study Law. He worked with the Fiji government and took part in the first world war on behalf of the British forces. He introduced many far reaching reforms in Fiji.)

Meanwhile, in India on January 9, 1917 a great demonstration was held at Allahabad, being the first massive public campaign against the indentured labor system. The gathering was addressed by Pandit Motilal Nehru and one of the memorable speeches on the occasion was that of Mrs. Sarojini Naidu who appealed to the men to put an end to the humiliation of Indian women in the colonies.

Massive meetings then took place all over the country, and the movement filtered down from the elite to the very grassroots of the Indian society. The momentum reached a crescendo when Mahatma Gandhi decided to make it the first test of the Satyagraha (which had been so successful in South Africa) by announcing that unless the system was ended, he would start picketing all emigrant ships.

On March 12, 1917, the Government of India stopped all recruitment to the colonies as a special measure under the Defence of India Act for the duration of the First World War and for two year afterwards.

On January 1, 1920, all indentures in Fiji were cancelled. The system came to an end but the deep wounds it left behind were still in evidence more than five decades later.

V

CHAPTER

My Father in His Father's Land

"Arise, awake and stop not until the goal is reached."

Swami Vivekananda

Bere Singh, like his father before him, returned to his native village Jaingara after a 16 year stint in the Fijian civil service. He took premature retirement ostensibly on health grounds. He suffered with asthma which is seriously aggravated when the cane flowers and sheds it allergenic pollen. However, the real reason was his constant confrontations with the racial prejudices prevalent in colonial Fiji.

Earlier, Bere Singh had returned home in 1916 for a year-long sabbatical from Fiji. His eldest son, Bhagwan Singh, was born during that long home leave. Bhagwan Singh was a baby when his father returned to Fiji. He grew up hearing stories of a distant land called Fiji where his grand-parents, Ram Chandar and Padam Kaur, had gone to work and his father Bere Singh was born.

When the young Bhagwan Singh saw his father for the first time at the tender age of nine years he felt shy. His own father was a stranger and he hid behind his grandmother. There was a sense of awe with which he regarded his father. He was returning from his *matra bhumi*; not India but Fiji, the land about which he had heard much about as he lay in the comforting arms of his grandmother because his grandmother had many stories to tell.

She was not bitter about her battles for justice for her husband grievously wronged by a system stacked against the disempowered. She told him stories about the natural beauty and abundance of this far away land. She recounted the kindness and love which had endeared her to many in her times of trouble. She would jokingly say that his own father was but a suckling babe secure in her bosom during those times of heartbreaking trauma.

That deep sense of self respect, inherited from his grandparents Ram Chandar and Padam Kaur and his own father, Bere Singh, was deeply ingrained in Bhagwan Singh as well. Jats are a proud people but this family was imbued with special values. They had seen hardship, endured family disputes, struggled through cultural upheaval, survived an inhumane journey into slavery, endured the ignominy of the "girmit", fought false imprisonment for arson and then finally gained reprieve and justice. They had been through many tests which mould character and resolve. They came out resilient but without rancour.

There is little doubt that the struggles of his grandparents and father left a deep impression on Bhagwan Singh, my father. In his memory, the family's struggles were not so much about the suffering caused by the tribulations but more about what these sufferings had taught them. They were the ingredients which would mould a view of life imbued in pragmatism, adaptability, a strong self belief and optimism. Not surprisingly, his was an eventful life, capped off by his stint as India's first High Commissioner to Fiji.

His early years played a very formative role in his later success as an administrator and diplomat, roles in which his many and varied skills, interests and knowledge — developed in school and college — had a significant bearing on how well he carried out his responsibilities. Almost from the time that he could exercise choice, my father was one who embraced life with enthusiasm and humility.

His life long love for Urdu and his innate appreciation of Urdu poetry he imbibed early in life from his maternal grandfather, Munshi Kanhaiya Lal, who was the Aalim-Fazil (widely respected for his knowledge of Urdu) of his village. This was even before his father, in his pursuit of "modernising" his son, admitted him into Victoria High School in Agra and made him the youngest boarder, at 11 years, at Jat House, the same facility where Bere Singh had boarded and befriended Sir Chhotu Ram.

At Victoria High, English was the lingua franca and his initial alienation from the language he directed towards an association with the independence movement swirling around him. He was 13 when he was briefly suspended from school for leading a group of students to meet with Mahatma Gandhi, who spent nine days in Agra in 1929.

He was a little older when he developed an interest in the heart-rending and tear-jerking narratives of the Waqiyat-e-Karbala (The Battle for Karbala, about the martyrdom of the Prophet's grandson, Ali), at the all-night "Majlises" at the residences of the city's prominent Shia families. This he did by slipping out of the iron gates of the hostel at night and slipping back before dawn, with a liberal supply of "khajoors" (dates) in hand.

Around this time he also developed an avid interest in Islamic history under the influence of Dr. Agha Mehdi Hasan, a renowned historian. He also became a regular listener of the intensely nationalistic religious speeches of the "Ahrar" leaders (who opposed the then nascent partition sentiment), particularly Maulana Aftab Ullah Shah Bukhari and Habib-ur-Rahman Ahrari, sitting through many all night meetings addressed by the two leaders on the roof of the shoe market at Hing-ki-Mandi. Those days Agra's famous shoe industry was almost 100 per cent owned and manned by Muslims.

Headier still were his years at Agra College, where his crowning achievement was to win the election to the presidency of the students' union in 1938. In college, there was not a single mass movement that he did not throw himself into at a time when the nation was in a turmoil all of which, as he noted in his memoirs, drew him into "deeper and deeper into everything else except text books".

In 1941, having done his MA in History from Agra University, he opted, on the advice of Sir Chhotu Ram (perhaps the most influential Jat leader of that time), to join the British Indian Army as an Indian Commissioned Officer. He served in the north-west frontier through much of the War, with the most memorable posting as the SSO at Waziristan, deep in Pashtun territory.

Then came another twist of fate: in 1944 he was selected for the Indian Civil Service from the war reserved vacancies category. This was a prestigious opening for only a select few and led to a series of senior posts in what later became the Indian Administrative Service.

It is common for Indian civil servants to handle diverse responsibilities in their careers but even by those standards, my father's diversity of assignments was perhaps more than most. His first assignment was to assist T N Kaul, then of the ICS and later in the foreign service and India's foreign secretary, in the selection of other ICS officers against the war-reserved vacancies.

This was followed soon after by being made the District Collector of Bulandshahr the year after partition. Bulandshahr was a communally sensitive district with a large Muslim population, many of them wealthy landlords, and a volatile mix of prominent agricultural communities of Jats, Rajputs and Gujjars. The district saw large scale migrations too, both to and from Pakistan, and it would have required only a small spark to light the cauldron. But my father's deft handling ensured that there was not a single communal incident in the district.

He had been in the service for less than a decade when his services were transferred to the centre where he remained till he quit the service on being made the High Commissioner to Fiji in 1971. Among his many assignments his longest stint was as Chairman of the Tea Board in Calcutta. And among his most high-profile stint was as the Commissioner for Delhi (when there was a common commissioner for what is now split into Delhi Municipal Corporation and the New Delhi Municipal Corporation).

Through those years, one of the threads that was woven into all his professional responsibilities was curiosity about Fiji. The family lore was substantial enough despite my grandfather's active discouragement of display of any interest in Fiji by his son. When my father found the classic on Fiji, "Fiji Mein Mere Ikkis Varsh" (My Twenty One Years in Fiji) by Tota Ram Sandhya among his father's papers, he read it several times away from his father's gaze.

After he finished school he urged his father to pursue his Fiji fixation, so the worried father took him to meet Rev. CF Andrews, who gave him the same advice as his father: "Complete your higher education; there will be many opportunities for educated young men in India." He was not fully convinced at the time but he accepted it; he only realised the full value of the counsel when he finally made it to Fiji as a diplomat.

His obsession with Fiji lay dormant till 1950 when he met Pandit Raghavanand a friend of his father and one of the senior most Indian Civil servants in Fiji, who was returning from London with his sister, Saraswati Devi. They stayed with my father at the Deputy Commissioner's House in Rai Bareilly in Uttar Pradesh where they had long conversations about the historical association my family had with Fiji.

Six months later Mr. Odin Ramarkha, another friend of his father from the Fiji Colonial Civil Service days, stayed with Bhagwan Singh for a month along with his wife and son. The wide gaps in the long and chequered account of my family's association with Fiji started getting filled.

In 1953, after my father had already shifted to Delhi, three more visitors came from Fiji who were returning from London on their way to Fiji. Most prominent among them was Pandit Vishnu Deo, an Indian member of what was then known as the Legislative Council of Fiji, and a close friend of my grandfather. He was accompanied by Mr. J.P. Maharaj, a prominent and propertied businessman of Suva, and a leading farmer, Thakur Jang Bahadur Singh. At the dinner my father hosted for them at Nirula's, where my grandfather joined them, Pandit Vishnu Deo left the strongest impression with his simplicity and honesty of purpose.

My father's interest in Fiji turned into a virtual obsession when Pandit Raghavanand and his wife re-visited India, going around the world by sea in 1958, and stayed with him at Calcutta where he was stationed by the Rehabilitation Ministry to which he was then attached. The redoubtable Dharam Vira, Secretary (Rehabilitation), used to visit Calcutta regularly every quarter. The Raghavanands were guests of my father on one of Dhatam Vira's visits.

Mrs. Raghavanand, popularly known as 'Badki Amma' (Elder Mother), cooked chicken and meat in the Fiji style for him, which Dharam Vira really relished. 'Badki Amma" cornered Dharam Vira one day and asked him since he was such a big man in India, could he not post Bhagwan Singh as India's Commissioner in Fiji.

Dharam Vira laughed and turned to my father and asked how such a thing could be done. "You are too senior to be made a Commissioner." At that time, the Indian representation in Fiji was through a Commissioner, a relatively junior post.

When his first attempt to get a posting to Fiji came to nought, my father thought that was the end of his Fiji obsession. He knew he could not visit Fiji on his own as the savings of an IAS officer in those days were not enough for him to indulge in the luxury of a holiday in far off Fiji.

Then, unexpectedly, two opportunities to visit Fiji came in quick succession. He was the commissioner, MCD, in 1965 when Air-India invited him to their inaugural commercial flight to Fiji. Two years later, as Chairman, Tea Board, he made a trip to Australia to promote Indian tea and extended it to visit Fiji. On both these trips he renewed friendships seeded by his father. Bere Singh's associates were now influential and he met many of them, none more important than Ratu Kamisese Mara, then Chief Minister of Fiji.

The Kamisese Mara connection was to prove very significant for my father. As he wrote in his memoirs: "It was about 7-8 months later (after the trip to Fiji) that I got a telephone call at my headquarters at Calcutta from Minister Dinesh Singh at New Delhi that I should join a dinner hosted by him for the Chief Minister of Fiji the next day. I was thrilled. Those days there was only one Calcutta-Delhi flight via Nagpur. This all night flight to Delhi added up to the excitement. I was happy to meet again the Chief Minister Ratu K. K. T. Mara and his wife Adi Lala. (He was not till then knighted). My most important gain from this dinner meeting was the friendship I built with Adi Mara which has lasted all these years. And later, whenever I had some small problems in Fiji, Adi Mara was most helpful".

In November 1970, immediately after Fiji's independence, Ratu Sir Kamisese Mara, now the Prime Minister, and his wife, accompanied amongst others, by the Leader of the Opposition, Mr. S. M. Koya and his wife, Amina, visited India. By now, my father was an Additional Secretary in the Ministry of Foreign Trade. At the Rashtrapati Bhavan pre-dinner session, the Fijian delegation cracked a joke that in case at any time the Indian Government found Bhagwan Singh missing from India, they could always trace him in Fiji where he really belonged.

This was overheard by the then Foreign Secretary T. N. Kaul, his old friend from the Federal Public Service Commission days in 1945-46. A few days later, Mr. Kaul spoke to my father to say that in case he was interested in going to Fiji as High Commissioner this was the time since Fiji was now an independent country. My father explained the background of the joke to him and immediately sent him a letter offering his services.

When P.N. Haksar, then Principal Secretary to the Prime Minister Indira Gandhi, heard of his family's past association with Fiji he thought my father would be an ideal choice for heading the Indian Mission there. Mr. Haksar remarked to my father when they met, "I knew you as the fire eating student leader of Agra; I never imagined you were a 'Prabasi Bharatiya' (Overseas Indian)."

Prime Minister Indira Gandhi approved his transfer to the External Affairs Ministry as "Officer-on-special Duty"- an administrative anachronism used to tide over many an ad hoc situation. This was an interim arrangement till all formalities for the announcement of his appointment as High Commissioner to Fiji were completed.

As has been said, when something has to happen the Fates conspire to make it happen. Ram Chandar was a "girmitiya", his Fiji-born son had served in the Fijian civil service and now some 80 years later Bhagwan Singh was to become the envoy of the largest democracy in the world to the youngest and perhaps the smallest new nation. For Bhagwan Singh this was a mission of the heart and a tryst with destiny.

His appointment was equally emotional for the people of Indian descent in Fiji. That the progeny of one of the "girmityas" had risen from the coolie lines to now occupy the prestige and residence in India House gave them a deep sense of pride. No surprise then that when my father landed at Suva, he was received by hundreds of people led by Pandit Raghavanand and his sister Saraswati.

Bhagwan Singh was perceived as "one of us" by the Indian community. They would be filled with joy and wonder whenever he spoke of the family history and his life experiences. He had an authentic Fijian heritage and could relate the "girmit" experience with stories of hardship and injustice which could not be matched. He was a powerful and entertaining speaker in English and Hindi and well versed in Urdu poetry. He soon became a favourite chief guest or guest speaker at public events. The 'son' was on show.

Fiji in the 1970s

The Fiji of my father's time was the closest to paradise. The Fijian Reef, second in the world after Australia's Great Barrier Reef, served as an introduction to the treasure house of beauty that Fiji was. As he wrote in his memoirs: "I was deeply moved by the beauty of these reefs. The profusion of coral shelters some unique marine life as well as provides a bountiful supply of food for its people."

He was also struck by the islands' abundant vegetation, perhaps one of the most striking aspects of Fiji. The islands had approximately 3,000 species of plants, of which just over a third were native to Fiji. The Bird of Paradise and the Crab Claw grew wild as did exotic orchids and the flamboyant Poinciana and of course the Hibiscus, Fiji's national flower. Fiji's most famous flower, however, was the 'tagimoucia', considered to be an extremely rare flower. Much more than perhaps anywhere else in the world, flowers play a vital role in the lives of the local people.

When Fiji became Independent in 1970, its total population was a little more than half a million, with Indians comprising a slight majority. The descendants of the "girmitiyas" in Fiji had progressed upward through education and entered different professions including lawyers, doctors, teachers and even politics besides the trade and commerce.

However, the two communities, the native Fijians and the Indian immigrants, led separate lives without much interaction with each other as the British colonial administration had deliberately kept the two major ethnic communities apart. The Fijians lived in the Mataqali or their traditional villages while the Indians were scattered on their leased farms and small settlements or in towns where they were involved in trading and business. But, importantly, both communities lived in peace.

On the eve of its independence, however, there was a deep sense of disquiet among ethnic Fijians about the Indian majority because of the democratic system of governance that Fiji was to adopt. Ethnic Fijians were apprehensive that the Fiji Indians would form a government on the strength of their vote one day. When that would happen, they feared, Fijians would lose their exclusive control over the land and resources of the country which they felt belonged primarily to them.

It did not help their disquiet that ethnic Indians got two major economic boosts in the 1970s. First the Lord Denning Award of 1970 gave them a minimum support price for their sugarcane produce. Then their land leases were renewed for periods ranging from 10 to 15 years. Some economists treat this period of the 1970s and early 80s as the golden period for the Indian farmers in particular and Fiji in general.

Work on the system of checks and balances between the two communities which independent Fiji would have begun with a 1965 constitutional conference held in London to negotiate a deal between the two major ethnic groups. The final Constitution document adopted at the conference expanded the voting franchise, previously restricted to Europeans and selected Indians and ethnic-Fijians.

Voters were classified according to ethnicity: Fijian, Indian, or General, (non-Fijian, non-Indian ethnicity). Legislative representatives were to be elected from the Indian and Fijian rolls. Land rights guaranteed by the Deed of Cession were given constitutional protection.

Crucially, Fijian chiefs were given an effective veto in all important matters affecting the status of Fijians and in changes to the Constitution itself. The Constitution gave power to Fijian politicians so long as they remained in partnership with the general voters and, critically, so long as the Fijian vote remained unified.

The final shape of Fiji's governance structure was spelt out in the Independence Constitution of 1970. A parliamentary system was established; with a Governor-General representing the Queen of England as Head of State. Fiji was to have a bicameral legislature: a House of Representatives, with a membership of 52, which was elected by ethnic roll call and a Senate that was appointed.

In the Senate, seven members were appointed by the Prime Minister, six by the leader of the opposition, eight by the Great Council of Chiefs (a purely Fijian body), and one by the Council of Rotuma. The appointment procedure to the Senate meant that ethnic Fijians would almost be guaranteed a majority.

Native Fijian leadership was founded on the feudal hierarchy of the indigenous Fijian society with half-a-dozen 'Tuis' holding sway over the main Fiji Islands. 'Tuis' were paramount chiefs with vast power over the people in their areas. Nominally, Tuis were elected, although only those of noble birth were eligible, and their tenure normally ran through a lifetime. Incidentally, there was no discrimination between the sexes for this high office. The 'Tui' of Vuya, an elderly and distinguished lady, was a living example.

The prefix 'Ratu' with the name of a person indicates a man of noble birth. Fiji's first prime minister, Ratu Kamisese Kapaiwai Tuimacilai Mara to give his full name, was born in the south-eastern Lau island group into an aristocratic family with Tongan and Samoan connections. He held the titles of Tui Lau, Tui Nayau and Sau Ni Vanua, an impressive pedigree reinforced by his wife's chiefly rank in her home island of Viti Levu.

But KKT Mara, as he used to sign his name, was, strictly speaking, not the highest chief of Fiji. The Vunivalu of Bau, Ratu Sir George Cakobau was considered the highest in the hierarchy of Chiefs, being the direct descendent of the Tui Viti (King of Fiji), the great Cakobau of Bau. Not surprisingly, there was a historical competition for supremacy in Fiji between the Tui of Lau and the King of Bau.

This devolved into a feeling of competitiveness between Tui Lau (Ratu Mara), who became Fiji's first Prime Minister and the Vunivalu of Bau (Ratu George Cakobau), who was independent Fiji's first Governor-General. Before independence, Ratu George was considered a diehard conservative chief as opposed to Ratu Mara's liberalism. But, as my father wrote, "I personally feel that Ratu George was more sinned against than sinning so far as Fiji Indians were considered."

In the Indian community most prominent in pre-independent Fiji were towering personalities like Pandit Badri Maharaj, Pandit Vishnu Deo and the fiery father figure of the National Federation Party (NFP), A.D. Patel. Patel's baton was picked up by Siddique (Sid) Koya, the aggressive and dynamic Leader of the Opposition in independent Fiji. A Bar-at-Law from Tasmania University in Australia, Koya took his work in every field very seriously.

H. M. Lodhia, a prominent businessman from Nadi and a popular member of the Federation Party since the A. D. Patel days, was a friend of my father who took every opportunity to discuss with him economic trends in the south Pacific, India and the world. It was he who brought the Ramakrishna Mission and its Fiji Head Swami Rudrananda close to my father. Swami Rudrananda the political monk had considerable hold both on Gujarati businessmen and sugarcane farmers.

Religious organisations have always played a very important role among ethnic Indians, irrespective of the community they belonged to. The Fiji Muslim League was a well-knit socio-religious organisation amongst whom the Shirani brothers of Suva and Shujaullah of Lautoka could be mentioned particularly.

The Arya Samaj was another such organisation with Pandit Raghavanand as its long-standing president while its mahila (women's) wing was headed by his sister, Saraswati Devi. Its greatest contribution to Fiji society was the numerous educational institutions run by it all over the country. It was ably managed by Dr. Ram Lakhan and Mr. Parameshwar.

Another great philanthropist of the time was Pandit Sridhar Maharaj, father of Shiromani, who rose from being a humble priest's son to build the biggest transport business in the country. He was associated with the Sanatan Dharam Sabha through his life, being its president for 16 years.

Christians amongst the Indians were also an influential group. My father's greatest friend amongst them was James Shanker Singh, at one time President of the Indian Alliance, a Cabinet Minister and the closest Indian ally of Prime Minister Ratu Mara. James was the son of Jung Bahadur Singh, who had visited my father in Calcutta.

The greatest Hindi novelist of Fiji was undoubtedly Joginder Singh Kamal, Principal, Khalsa College at Ba. His descriptions of the human struggles during the indenture period were particularly absorbing. Pandit Kamla Prasad Mishra who ran the Hindi weekly *Jai Fiji* and was fluent in Sanskrit, Arabic, Hindi, Urdu, Persian and English, was also considered to be an outstanding poet of international standards.

The other literary friend of my father in Fiji was Pandit Guru Dutt Sharma, Editor of *Shanti Dhoot* the Hindi weekly published by the *Fiji Times*. A prominent social worker of long standing, he was also a Hindi writer of considerable repute. Also influential in my father's time were three relatively young authors - Subramani Satendra, P. Nandan and Ahmed Ali - all talented lecturers of the University of the South Pacific with the latter two also being members of the Parliament.

No description of the Indian political scene will be complete without mentioning the role of another irrepressible barrister, Sir Vijay R. Singh, the first Fiji Indian to be knighted. A close associate and easily the ablest political ally of Ratu Mara, he acted as the Prime Minister's aide in various international conferences and a strategist in the domestic scene. However, he fell out with Ratu Mara later and joined the opposition.

In the judiciary too, Indians had two outstanding figures. With both these figures my father had close familial relationships. Sir Moti Tikaram was the first Indian to become a Judge of the Supreme Court and on occasions even officiated as the Chief Justice. He then became the first Ombudsman of Fiji. The other was Justice Ghananand Mishra. A nephew of Pandit Raghavanand, he was one of the more illustrious Mishra brothers and was widely considered one of the ablest legal minds to have entered the highest court of Fiji. Unlike the gregarious, outgoing social Sir Moti, Justice Ghananand was a very private person who adhered to the British tradition of a judge maintaining his distance from people.

The Indian representation in Fiji was set up in 1949 as a diplomatic post in recognition of the fact that even though it was still a British colony, its majority population was of Indian origin and the government of newly independent India recognised that it needed to have a post in Fiji to specifically look after their welfare.

However, when Fiji became independent in 1970, the same mission had to change its orientation and to represent India to both the communities. A P Venkateswaran, one of the IFS' ablest officers (who, unfortunately, will be most remembered in history as the Foreign Secretary who was fired at a press conference by Prime Minister Rajiv Gandhi) was the Commissioner when Fiji attained independence. He stayed on for a few months as the putative High Commissioner and began the process of re-orienting the role of the Indian representation.

The new political thrust of the mission was not popular with the descendants of the "girmitiyas": from the friend-philosopher of the Indians in Fiji to become the friend of the indigenous Fijians -the 'Kaivitis' - was a half about-turn. It did not help my father that the Fiji media had labelled him as a Fiji-born High Commissioner, (which actually he was not), thus raising the expectations and enthusiasm of the Indo-Fijians.

This was the first and foremost challenge before him. As a representative of India he was supposed to interact with all the communities of Fiji when, in fact, the iTaukei or the ethnic Fijian community historically had had little or no interaction with the Indians.

The mission was also acutely short-staffed, the highest officer being an Attache (akin to a Section Officer in the Indian Government). The Australian and the New Zealand trading community looked at him askance when they came to know that his previous assignment was in the Ministry of Foreign Trade (and not the Foreign Ministry). To them his posting spelt danger.

He also had to deal with the other neighbouring countries of accreditation, the Kingdom of Tonga and the Republic of Nauru, and through them all had to establish a connect with the entire South Pacific island nations who were important for India at international forums, particularly the United Nations.

With all these challenges the two greatest supporting factors worked in his favour were his service with the Army in the Second World War and the family connections with Fiji. Above all was the word that went round that he knew Ratu Mara personally and had met him in India much before he became the first Prime Minister of independent Fiji.

In Suva, after he had his initial round of official meetings, he slowly began his outreach to the indigenous Fijians. A good judge of people, he saw an opportunity when he saw a small statue of Ratu Sukuna in a park in the heart of Suva's main market. He was aware of the standing of Ratu Sakuna in Fijian society.

Ratu Sir Josefa Lalabalavu Vana'ali'ali Sukuna, to give his full name, was to Fiji what Gandhi was to India. Popularly known as Lala Sukuna, he was the eldest child of the former Tui Nayau - the paramount chief of the Bau Group of islands. He died in 1958.

April 22 is the birth anniversary of Ratu Sukuna. On that day in 1972 he, accompanied by Pandit Raghavanand, my father's friend who had also been a friend of Ratu Lala Sukuna, reached the park unannounced to pay floral tributes to the great Fijian chief. As this was lunch time and the peak shopping period, they were soon surrounded by a huge crowd of curious onlookers. They left quietly after paying their respects.

Nai Lalakai, a Fijian language weekly, in its next issue came out with an editorial heaping praise on this simple act. My father wrote, "This act of ours brought me two unexpected dividends: my standing with the common Fijian sky-rocketed, and I made many life-long friends in the community. Amongst them was Ratu Luke, an ardent admirer of Ratu Sukuna and the editor of *Nai Balakai* who often referred to this incident as an example to others."

My father toured extensively. He did not believe that his diplomatic role should confine him to his office. The lack of staff did not deter him. He travelled by road, sea and air, on horseback, canoes and outboard motor launches to remote islands to reach villages and communities. His black Mercedes car flying the Indian tricolour could often be seen bouncing along on the dirt roads to isolated rural Indian settlements.

He thought nothing of wading through the slushy mud at low tide to reach an island village. He was comfortable sitting on the floor on a pandanus mat during the long, elaborate Fijian tribal welcomes. The Fijians responded to his enthusiastic desire to reach out to them with the High Chiefs inviting him to their village festivities. There he spoke amongst other things about Indian cottage industries which generated income for their communities.

During one of his road trips to a school near the farming town of Ba, my father learnt something about his own father. He met an elderly school teacher named Wahab at the Lal Bahadur Shastri School. Wahab tentatively asked him about his family history. When he was told my grandfather's name, he became very excited, saying that he had been like a father figure to him.

Wahab explained that when Babu Bere Singh was living in Ba, he would often ride out on his horse to visit friends and would stop on the way at a tea shop run by Wahab's father. Babu Bere Singh had not only encouraged Wahab to study but also provided him with books and helped him with his English lessons. It was an emotional moment for my father to meet a person who had known his father and respected him so deeply.

There were many others who also remembered Bere Singh. They said Bere Singh was known to be the best dressed Indian of his time in Fiji. It was a side of his father that Bhagwan Singh had never known but he now understood his own attraction to suave dressing.

The Fiji army was dominated by indigenous Fjians. Few Indians met the physical requirements. There was also some negativity about the army amongst the Indian community. Indians were rarely if ever invited to army functions. But Bhagwan Singh was an exception. My father had served as a British Indian Army Officer during the war.

He was a welcome guest at the Army Mess. To forge the ties of army camaraderie he presented a silver replica of a uniformed soldier of his own regiment, the Rajputana Rifles on behalf of the Indian Ex-Servicemen's League to the mess. Not surprisingly he was made an honorary member of the Officers Mess at the Queen Elizabeth Barracks of the Fiji Military Forces.

My father was often invited to the Officers Mess by the Commander of the Fiji Military Forces, Col. Paul Manueli. They were often joined by the deputy Prime Minister Ratu Sir Edward Cakobau, who had seen active duty in Malaya during WW II. I sometimes tagged along with my father to these beer sessions.

I always found their mess culture somewhat amusing. They would stand ramrod stiff but quaintly the right knee always seemed slightly bent. The mess atmosphere was very British and typical of the country's colonial past shared throughout the then Commonwealth. The mess sessions were filled with nostalgia reminiscences and of old army jokes.

I was under strict instructions from my father to be in attendance to Ratu Sir Edward when he came to India House. The charming and good looking Ratu Edward had a special position in Fijian society. He was a high chief of Fiji and closely related to the King of Tonga. Whilst the Ratu rank carries prestige and precedence it also requires the title holder not to flaunt his position or show any arrogance. Ratu Edward was always dignified, affable, quietly spoken, benevolent and much respected.

My father was an early pioneer of soft diplomacy, much before Joseph Nye articulated the concept of soft power in international relations. He was instrumental in establishing the first ever Indian Cultural Centre (ICC) abroad in Suva under the auspices of the Indian Council of Cultural Relations ICCR). Inaugurating it, Fijian Prime Minister Ratu Mara said,

> "The people of Fiji are all Fiji citizens whatever their origin. This is a good portent of the future success of the centre. We are a multi-racial community and the more we can understand each other's cultures, the more we will learn to understand each other."

The ICC provided lessons in classical music and dance. They had teachers for both instrumental and vocal music and dance teachers of Bharatnatyam and Kathak. The Centre had an immediate impact. Singing and dancing was an essential part of Fijian life, but the Fijians had never seen anything like the Indian classical art forms. They were fascinated by Indian dancers.

The Indian community in Fiji is a traditional and deeply religious community. Religion and cultural practices had helped maintain the Indian identity through the hardship of the plantation days. For the Indians, the presentation of Indian culture was a source of deep pride.

The visiting artists did not stay restricted to the Cultural Centre but often gave demonstration performances in schools, local open air gatherings and social and cultural events. At times of natural calamities, like hurricanes and floods, the Centre held performances to raise funds for relief work. As Ratu Mara had said, the Centre aided the understanding between cultures, not only within Fiji but the other Pacific island nations as well.

Over the years, Bhagwan Singh, an ardent admirer of the ghazal, found ways to invite famous singers and qawali troupes as well as folk artistes to tour Fiji. Phag (holi) performers were a particular hit among the Indian farming community which observes the phag festival enthusiastically though in a more gentle fashion than the north Indian holi.

The Cultural Centre held special Hindi classes and presented Hindi books to schools around the country and the University of the South Pacific. Through the Centre, musical instruments were gifted to bhajan mandalis. Copies of the Ramayana, Gita, Mahabharat were presented to organisations like the Sanatan Sabha, the Arya Samaj and Sangam.

His second instrument of soft diplomacy was the scholarship schemes of the ICCR and the Commonwealth and Indian Technical and Economic Cooperation programmes. He made such selections that created a strong alumni in Fiji, drawn from both communities, among influential sections like doctors, engineers, government officers and journalists.

When Bhagwan Singh got an extension in service at the end of his tenure of three years as High Commissioner the *Fiji Times* brought out a special supplement dated May 30, 1975. Among the write-ups in the supplement was a column listing the 52 beneficiaries of different scholarship schemes in which they were sent for studies in India. Many of them were in the senior levels of Fiji's establishment when I arrived in Suva as the new Indian High Commissioner in 2005.

Most of the doctors on that list had migrated to greener pastures in Australia, New Zealand and America. But there were many who remained in positions of influence including the Foreign Secretary, several permanent secretaries, members of Parliament, educationists and university academics. Amongst the many there was a Fijian woman executive heading a wildlife related UN office in Suva. They were a great source of goodwill for me personally when I was the Indian High Commissioner almost four decades later. The large group of alumni of Indian institutions in Fiji has remained well disposed towards India.

The Pacific leaders had already been impressed by the Indian offer to upskill doctors holding diplomas from the Fiji School of Medicine, the only medical institution in the region. My father had organised a programme through which those doctors could attend a special two-year condensed course at Mysore Medical College to obtain a graduate degree in medicine. India was not in a position to match Australia and New Zealand, the two main donors in the region, and had to target its offers of assistance to more effective and useful programmes.

My father's wide range of interests and his long years in government had helped him develop a vast network of friends and colleagues. He was always on the lookout for inviting Indians of influence in a variety of fields to visit Fiji and share their expertise. He would try to persuade

Indians visiting Australia – whether senior officials, businessmen, writers, sportsmen and others - to extend their tours to Fiji. The aim was to showcase different aspects of Indian life. The distance between India and Fiji and India's leading role in the global de-colonisation movement had made communication difficult before Fiji's independence, resulting in a lack of knowledge about India in Fiji, even among Indians.

However, this outreach did not endear my father to the Indian diplomatic establishment. One such example was his reaching out to the Indian naval chief that caused some heartburn in South Block. When he heard on the grapevine that an Indian naval ship would be in this part of the world, he wrote to the naval chief who was an old friend from his army days and inquired whether Fiji could be included in the goodwill tour. The naval headquarters and the Ministry of Defence approved the tour to Fiji and this was reluctantly cleared by the External Affairs Ministry.

The goodwill visit of the INS Betwa was a resounding success. INS Betwa, an anti-aircraft frigate sailed into Suva Harbour in the morning on June 7, 1976. The sight of the Indian naval ship flying the Indian flag and pennants fluttering in the sea breeze gladdened the heart of the Indian community.

The next day was an open day and both Indians and Fijians queued up to go on board the war ship. The Betwa's band gave a performance at the Ratu Sukuna park that wowed their audience and heavily built Fiji maramas (ladies) got up to dance to the music.

One of the largest ever receptions was held at India House which was attended by the top Fiji leadership and the captain and senior officers of the ship. Next morning, my father and Captain Rishi Raj Sood made a courtesy call on Acting Prime Minister Ratu Penaia Ganilau. It was a special gesture on Ratu Penaia's part to acknowledge the first visit of an Indian naval ship in Fiji. From the moment the frigate was sighted in the outer reaches of the harbour till it sailed out, there was a constant crowd near the port gazing at the ship.

Sir Ratu Mara and Bhagwan Singh

Ratu Sir Kamisese Mara was tall, proud and cogitative. Educated at Oxford and London School of Economics, he stood out as a leader of men in any gathering. My father developed a good understanding with

Ratu Mara which soon evolved into an excellent rapport. Ratu Mara often invited Bhagwan Singh on his tours to outer islands. My father's long and varied administrative experience provided him the background to talk on subjects like village development, community enterprises, food processing and rural infrastructure. Ratu Mara came to value his suggestions and observations, many of which came with offers of Indian assistance.

Ratu Mara, as a high tribal chief and the popular leader of Fiji, was highly respected in the Pacific region. He was the architect of the Pacific Islands Forum, the regional organisation of the independent Pacific Island territories established in 1971. My father's congenial relations with Ratu Mara helped him establish a good equation with the leaders of the other Pacific nations to which he was accredited as High Commissioner, the Kingdom of Tonga, Western Samoa and the Republic of Nauru.

The conference of Pacific Island leaders brought together the leadership of the Pacific islands. One of its meetings was held in Suva. The Samoan Prime Minister's birthday was celebrated on one of the days of the conference with a traditional feast and the legendary Samoan dancers. Two days later, it was Ratu Mara's birthday and a Fijian lovo (earthen pit oven) was organised.

My father decided to have Indian artists perform at the birthday festivities; he quietly arranged it with Lady Mara. The Kathak performance and the duet between the sarod and the tabla players amazed the Pacific leaders. All of them congratulated Ratu Mara on the Indian performances. A simple gesture had made a memorable impact on the Pacific leaders and gratified Ratu Mara as well.

Ratu Mara and my father were popular figures for the media. Towards the later part of his tenure, the magazine, *Pacific Journal* published from Australia wrote that if there were to be a contest for the most photographed personality in the Pacific islands there would be a tie between Ratu Mara and Bhagwan Singh. It was a typically Australian comment tinged with mischief – India's relations with Australia in the days of its White Australia policy were not as friendly as they are today. No Prime Minister would care to be upstaged by a foreign diplomat.

Politicians and leaders are often sensitive about media reportage and an Indian media report put my father in a tricky situation with the Fiji Prime Minister. Ratu Mara was an admirer of Mahatma Gandhi and had read Jawaharlal Nehru's writings. He had a good equation with Indira Gandhi as co-leaders of the Commonwealth. He had keen interest in Indian political developments and regularly read Indian newspapers.

My father would send him some Indian periodicals every week and the *National Herald* in particular since it had a good section on foreign affairs. In those days the newspapers and mail arrived once a week in the diplomatic bag from Delhi. A problem arose in 1972 with the visit of an academic from India, which was related by my father in memoirs, "My Father's Land".

"It was in the year 1972 that one Prof. M.S. Rajan, of the Indian Council of World Affairs, was on a lecture tour in Australia. My colleague in Canberra telephoned to ask me whether I could invite Rajan to Fiji for about a week. He was to arrange his own airfare and I would be responsible for local hospitality. Prof. Rajan came and stayed with me, and Dr. Ishwar Chauhan, Director, Indian Cultural Centre, looked after his needs. But where Dr. Chauhan failed was that he could not arrange a meeting between him and Prime Minister Ratu Mara. I personally did not think it was necessary either. Rajan on return to India decided to write an article for the *National Herald*. Those days *National Herald* was the only paper which published features on Fiji.

One week when I opened the newspaper, I was shocked to see that the Professor had attacked and criticised the Prime Minister of Fiji for having kept a British Colonial Officer as his Foreign Secretary. This he construed as a contradiction in independent Fiji. The article was not happily worded either. For a moment I was stunned. I was certain that when Ratu Mara read it he would be upset.

Ratu Mara was known to be very sensitive about personalised attacks. I was advised that we should not send him that particular issue of *National Herald* but replace it by *Hindustan Times*. Mr. O P Dhawan, the Attaché, whose advice I always found extremely useful, suggested that I should keep other copies of this issue of the *National Herald* also in my own drawer. He argued that even if a single copy of it got out, someone was bound to bring it to the PM's notice.

Weeks passed by, nothing happened. I convinced myself that we had put the lid over an embarrassing situation. But soon in the duty-free shopping centre of Cumming Street, Suva (a prominent meeting place for a diversified sections of people in the capital) subdued whispers that somebody had managed to put a wedge between the PM and the Indian

High Commissioner could be heard. It did not take me long to put two and two together. Clearly the Prime Minister had somehow got to see the offending article and taken exception to it.

For days together, Dhawan and I discussed how to handle the situation. Since more than two months had passed, we decided we would wait to know the PM's reaction directly. About a week later, on a Friday afternoon, the telephone rang for me. It was the PM's Fijian Personal Assistant. PM was going to Lau islands that evening on his boat 'Degei' for the week-end. If I were free, he would like me to join him. Dhawan was quick to catch on. He pulled out the article from my drawer, gave it to me and said: "This is bound to come up for discussion".

This was not the first time that I had gone with Ratu Mara on his boat to the outer islands. But that evening the mode of invitation and its timing were somewhat intriguing. I collected my sleeping suit and shaving kit and put them in my briefcase with the favourite bottle also tucked in. I was received at the wharf by the captain of the 'Degei' and shown to my cabin. The Prime Minister had already come and occupied his own cabin. Soon the 'Degei' set sail.

We literally sailed into the setting sun. The hot sun made the blue water glimmer. Ratu Mara came out of his cabin and stood at the base of the mast, facing the sinking sun. I was the only other passenger. I too stepped out of my cabin and stood by his side. When he turned back there was a stern expression on his face. "Mr. High Commissioner, I would like to know what you and your country feel about me. You have been telling me that they have a certain opinion of me in India. But do you know what Pandit Nehru's own paper has written about me?"

The cat was out of the bag. It was no use putting up diplomatic pretences. I replied: "Sir, I know Prof. Rajan's article has been worrying you for the last few days but cannot understand how your Excellency could take a casual visitor's uninformed and unkind remarks so seriously." Ratu Mara was not mollified. "The point, Mr. High Commissioner, is that it is Nehru's paper and a professor who visited Fiji has been maligning me." I could see how deeply hurt he was. I pleaded that I had taken note of that and had already written to the External Affair Ministry and also to the editor of the *National Herald*. I said that I did not want to raise a public controversy. Ratu Mara continued to protest: "I don't think I deserved this treatment in the Indian press from someone who had enjoyed the Fijian hospitality, Mr. Fiji-born High Commissioner." There was a taunt in his tone.

I struck out for the last time: "Sir, we in India are used to such writings. There have been numerous instances where foreigners after visiting India for a few days, and enjoying our hospitality, saw nothing good in India. We just laugh at such things. There was a British lady, Miss Katherine Mayo, who came to India and wrote a book entitled 'Mother India' which was described by Mahatma Gandhi as a "Gutter Inspector's Report". If we had taken it seriously, the British and Indians could not have been as friendly and understanding as we are even after so many years of our independence. I plead with Your Excellency to ignore it and forget it. I do not have to give you proof of the esteem we in India hold you in."

As if this was not enough, I topped it by saying: "Since it has hurt Your Excellency's feelings, I am going to write a personal letter to this writer about this." I knew this verbal dispute could not stretch beyond this. The high traditions of the Chiefs of Fiji lay down strict rules of chivalry. Ratu Mara certainly was a high chief - 'Tui of Nayau and Tui of Lau'. The topic was buried deep down the Pacific Ocean along with the setting sun. He said in the typical British tradition in which he was educated: "The Sun has gone down; let us have a sun-downer."

"Bula Vinaka" (an all purpose greeting meaning wishing you happiness and good health) was my instant response!'

Fijians value their connection with the British crown, perhaps more than any other colony because they were not conquered by the British but their chiefs voluntarily ceded the Fiji Islands to Britain. This attachment did not cease with the independence of Fiji so in 1974, four years after independence, the Fijians decided to hold a grand celebration to mark the hundred years of Cession.

A section of Indians in Fiji took it as a celebration of the enslavement of Fiji because, while Fijians were indifferent to the idea of independence, Indians had been active in the demand for independence from Britain. Opposition leaders in Fiji of Indian origin were ambivalent about the celebrations but my father strongly recommended to the Indian government to send a senior leader to represent India at the event.

Prince Charles represented Her Majesty the Queen on the occasion. The Indian government sent Union Minister for Civil Aviation Babu Raj Bahadur, accompanied by his wife.

The main centennial function was held at the island of Bau, Fiji's most prominent island before the Cession, which is off the east coast of the Viti Levu, Fiji's largest island in which Suva is located. By the time the dignitaries were heading towards Bau Island, the tide was turning. Halfway across the passage to Bau island the boat carrying the Indian party ran aground in the mud. The sun was beginning to set so the Fijian escorts urged the passengers to try walking half a kilometer distance to the jetty.

My sister Shubha was part of the Indian group often and recounted what followed. My mother, Mrs. Raj Bahadur and Shubha hitched up their saris to walk in the shallow waters. A deep frown set in on Minister Raj Bahadur's face at this "shabby" treatment to the Indian representatives as he and my father struggled through the mud in their formal attire of churidar and achkan. But soon, they caught up with a group of Fijians wading across which included the Governor General, Ratu Sir George Cakobau, the Vunivalu, and his wife, Lady Lelea.

Ratu Sir George warmly greeted my father and walked along chatting with Babu Raj Bahadur in a friendly manner. Lady Lelea linked arms with my mother, Shubha and a young Fijian girl helped Mrs. Raj Bahadur. They waded through the waters as the accompanying group softly sang traditional Fijian songs to honour the chief and his guests. The Minister was mollified at the cheerful informality and accepted it as a unique experience. And a diplomatic incident was averted.

At the end of his three year tenure, it was time to pack our bags. My father's initial appointment was to end in 1974 and farewells had started in right earnest from the Fijian community, the Indian organisations, the Fiji government and the Fijian Armed Forces. He was all packed to go when Foreign Secretary Kewal Singh wrote to him to convey the appreciation of the Indian Prime Minister for bringing the Fijian and Indian communities together and the news of the extension of his tenure by a year.

History repeated itself in 1975 when he got the news of his second extension from the government of India after attending farewell parties for almost a month. Both *Fiji Times* and *Fiji Sun* brought out special issues of their papers highlighting his work in Fiji. Some people even joked that it was futile to host farewell events for Bhagwan Singh as he was never going to leave Fiji. Finally, after the completion of his second extension and five years of living in Fiji, it was time to go.

The *Fiji Times* in its editorial date July 2, 1976 under the caption 'Envoy Leaves' wrote, "His Excellency Bhagwan Singh leaves Fiji today after years of active, lively and eloquent service to both the country he represented as High commissioner, India and equally to Fiji, the country with which he has such strong familial ties.... He has cared deeply about Fiji in particular and the Pacific in general. It is to be hoped that we do not entirely lose touch."

In a message to the readers of *Fiji Times*, Bhagwan Singh said, "I have a relationship of sorts with the readers of *Fiji Times* which began in 1964 when I was subjected to both the journalistic interrogation and the photographic expertise of the then editor Mr. Len Usher. Even before my arrival in Fiji as Indian High Commissioner, the readers of this great national daily had gotten acquainted with me as a Fiji Born High Commissioner. Now when I prepare to emplane, I can not help but reflect that my family history seems to have come full circle at a crucial stage of this great nation's history.... Today, when I am being showered with affection and regard, it makes me conscious of my shortcomings. I only wish I could have done more."

"The other day I was completely swept off my feet when the Great Council of Chiefs farewelled me by presenting a Tabua at a special lunch hosted at the Soqosoqo Vakamarama Fijian Women's Association. I find words inadequate to convey my feelings. I, therefore, resort to the most effective, deeply felt words of thanks and I can only say Vinaka vakalevu." (Thank you very much)

Overwhelmed by the kind of response he was getting, my father decided to hold an Open House on 30th June. People who had not been able to meet him as well as others who had met him already, streamed through India House through the day to greet him.

The next day, he drove down to Nadi on the Queen's Road and as the familiar black Mercedes car flying the Indian flag drove by, people waved and called out "Ni sa moce" (farewell). Present at the airport to see them off were Minister for Health Mr. James Shankar Singh and Mrs. Singh, and Member of Parliament Surendra Prasad and Mrs. Prasad.

Adi Merewalesi, the wife of the Tui Vuda, Senator Ratu Josaia Tavaiqia presented him with salusalu (Fijian garland of flowers and bark of the vau tree presented on special occasions). Prominent social worker in the western region, Bechu Prasad garlanded him. A large crowd had also gathered at the Nadi International airport to bid him goodbye (it was a time when there were few security concerns at airports).

On July 2, 1976, my father boarded the Air New Zealand flight to Auckland. My mother had left for Sydney the day before. Shubha and I stayed back for several months before returning separately to India. I stayed on in Suva for some time, got married and returned to Delhi with my bride, Shiromani.

My father in his own assessment of his career considered his tenure in Fiji as the most satisfying. He wrote in his biography, "My five years in Fiji were the most emotionally satisfying out of the 35 years I spent in the service of my Government." He elaborated: "It will be emphasizing the obvious to say that I enjoyed every minute of my stay in Fiji, and, I am sure, the people of Fiji - right up to the grassroots level - shared that delight. My own Prime Minister, Shrimati Indira Gandhi, appreciated my role in cementing the relationship between the two major ethnic groups of Fiji. And, as a bonus, granted me unprecedented awards of two extensions in the service of Fiji which was somewhat unpalatable to my colleagues in the Indian Foreign Service. This enabled me to act as the Dean of the growing diplomatic corps in Fiji."

A remark by Sir Ratu Mara more than a decade after my father's tenure ended speaks eloquently of the high regard my father had among Fiji's elite. T P Sreenivasan was the High Commissioner in Fiji when the 1987 coup resulted in the Commission being closed down. In an obituary of Sir Ratu Mara, TP wrote when he died in 2004, he related a conversation with Sir Ratu Mara at the venue of their common passion, the golf course: "True to form, he delivered a long monologue (while speaking to me) about how some Indian high commissioners had fallen into the trap of assuming the leadership of the Fiji Indians and urged me not to fall prey to that temptation. He spoke of exceptions like Bhagwan Singh and A P Venkateswaran and asked me to emulate their examples."

My father was a multi-faceted personality who had an outstanding tenure in Fiji where he cemented India-Fiji ties and raised India's profile in the South Pacific region. The Sydney based *Pacific Islands Monthly* once wrote tongue-in-cheek about him, "India's one-man band can be seen and heard at every island and atoll in the Pacific."

It was a hard act to follow. I could only share my apprehension with Shiro, who calmed me with the words: "Don't you worry, am I not there with you all the time?" That is what got me going.

VI

CHAPTER

The First Lady and India House

"But love your feet only because they walked upon the earth and upon the wind and upon the waters, until they found me."

Pablo Neruda

What do wives of diplomats do? This question is often asked. Are there any guidelines or duties assigned to them? Fact is, there are no specific duties assigned to diplomats' spouses though there are certain dos and don'ts prescribed. And yet, even though they do not have any defined responsibilities, they can make a significant contribution to their husbands' career.

Entertaining guests has always been an essential part of an ambassador's role and this task almost always becomes the responsibility of the lady of the house. Organising a fine dinner on an elegantly laid table with a tasty meal and good conversation is an art that requires a good deal of work.

Not all spouses of ambassadors are simply housewives these days. Many of them are highly successful professionals, working in different fields back home. But the spouses of the heads of missions are not supposed to take up a paid assignment in the country of the deployment of their spouse.

India and Fiji both have been part of the British Colonial Empire and the working of the wives of the Viceroys and the Provincial Governors had a great imprint on the working of the spouses of our administrative and diplomatic officers. While the specific role the wives played depended on the nature and background of the lady and her surroundings, most first ladies by convention associated themselves with charitable works, health care and poor relief.

My mother, Shanta Singh, was a typical Indian housewife. Born in a large farming family in Bharau village of Mathura district, she was a devout and religious person. But she had lived with my father through his various enthusiasms and life experiences, including living in a mud hut in the forests of Keonjhar when my father decided to personally supervise the setting up of a new iron ore mine in Kiriburu in Jharkhand!

Home schooled in the Bharau haveli, she spoke only a smattering of English, though she understood it quite well, with four growing children chattering away in the language. But she took to the new assignment in Suva with aplomb. My mother disarmed the Indian ladies of Suva by telling them she considered Fiji her "sasural" (parents-in-laws home) since my father would often say, "India is my motherland, and Fiji is my father's land" (the title of his memoirs).

Under my mother India House was an open house, warmly welcoming to all, whether for formal dinners and receptions, or for ladies' organisations seeking help to raise funds for their activities. Thus, she became the patron of the Poor Relief Society, the Stree Sewa Sabha and the Sikh Women's Association of Fiji; supported the Mahila Mandal, the ladies wing of the Arya Pratinidhi Sabha of Fiji; helped the YWCA and the International Women's Association raise funds; and took the lead in raising funds to procure an audiometer for the Crippled Children's School.

The *Fiji Sun* on March 10, 1976 published a picture on its front page with the caption, "There were women everywhere in the Suva Civic Auditorium last night for a cultural performance organised by the wife of the Indian High Commissioner, Mrs. Bhagwan Singh as a farewell gesture. The performers were Indian dancers and musicians from the Indian Cultural Centre in Suva. Mrs. Singh is due to leave Fiji next month when her husband goes on retirement leave. Others in the picture are (from left to right) Mrs. Va Toganivalu, Mrs. Allice Toganivalu, Mrs. Irene Jai Narayan, Mrs. Singh, and Mrs. Shree Dhar Maharaj."

Seated next to Mrs. Maharaj was her daughter Shiromani but the caption did not mention her name. Little did the reporter realise at that time that this young lady would, after 29 years, take the place of the first lady in the India House.

THERE were women everywhere in the Suva Civic Auditorium last night for a cultural performance organised by the wife of the Indian High Commissioner, Mrs Bhagwan Singh [fourth from left] as a farewell gesture. The performers were Indian dancers and musicians from the Indian Cultural Centre in Suva. Mrs Singh is due to leave Fiji next month when her husband goes on retirement leave. Others in the picture are [from left to right]: Mrs Va Toganivalu, Mrs Allice Toganivalu, Mrs Irene Jai Narayan, Mrs Singh, and Mrs Shree Dhar Maharaj.

Unlike my mother, Shiro was a working professional. Born and brought up in Suva as a third-generation child of a prosperous family of "girmitiya" background, she attended Suva's top girls' school, St. Joseph's School, and went to Delhi's elite Miranda House for her undergraduate studies. Once back in Fiji, she worked for five years with the Fiji civil service as a training officer for the government's senior officers' programme.

After we got married we shifted to Delhi where she initially worked with the Canadian and later the New Zealand High Commissions in New Delhi as a Consular Officer. She then joined the UK Government's aid wing, DFID, at the British High commission, her last full time job in India.

She resigned in 2005 before accompanying me to Fiji. In Suva, Shiro's first challenge was to redo India House so that it truly represented Indian tradition and culture. The Indian mission was closed down after the Indian High Commissioner was expelled following the first military coup in 1987. It was reopened only in 1999 after diplomatic relations between India and Fiji were restored. But the new High Commissioner, Prof. I S Chauhan, who had earlier worked in Suva as Director of the Indian Cultural Centre during my father's tenure, preferred to stay in rented accommodation while the India House was under repair.

Though we moved into a rented house hired by the mission after arriving in Suva in March 2005, for Shiro and I moving into India House was a top priority for several reasons. One, it was a symbol of Indian pride. Two, I had spent a lot of time there in my youth and seen it host top government functionaries, including the Governor-General and the Prime Minister, as also High Chiefs, diplomats and people from different walks of life. Three, it was where Shiro and I had got engaged in 1976.

India House was an imposing cream coloured colonnaded structure in the Art Deco style. Shiro researched its heritage and discovered that it was one of the three remaining buildings in Fiji of that style: the other two being the President's House, home of the Colonial Governors, and Borron House, a Fiji National Trust building now being used for state guests but for many years the residence of Ratu Sir Lala Sukuna, the "father" of Fiji.

India House had been constructed by a very successful and wealthy lawyer Robert Crompton in the 1930s. It was set in large gardens and located on a low hill so it commanded wonderful views of the Suva peninsula. One could see the sun rise on the eastern horizon and follow it to the west as it set behind the hills. It was purchased by the Indian government in 1960 and named India House and became the residence of the Indian government's representative.

For ethnic Indians in Fiji, India House had a special significance. I remember my father relating an anecdote about a leading Indian lawyer, Abdul Lateef, who had been a legal clerk to Crompton. Lateef had turned very emotional when he first visited India House and said, "Commissionah sahib, you do not understand what this means to me. When I used to come to this house with legal files, Crompton would meet me at the porch and dismiss me. I was never allowed into this house. Now I am proud to be welcomed here as an honoured guest. It shows how our world has changed. To see the India flag flying on India House fills us with a deep sense of pride."

We were eager to shift to India House at the earliest but everything had to be organised from scratch. Shiromani was a meticulous planner and she devoted the bulk of her time in the initial months to make sure that the redone India House would not just represent all major streams of Indian culture and civilisation but that all the arts, artefacts, furniture and furnishings would complement each other so the sum of the parts was greater than the whole. It was painstaking work to keep every minute detail in mind as she proceeded to order all items from India.

The furniture she chose was a harmonious combination of art deco sofas and tables and Indian style settees and chairs to go with the architecture of the house. Everything was draped in rich Indian textiles and together the interiors exuded elegance and style in a warm, welcoming ambience. Shiro wanted people visiting India House to experience India in some small way by appreciating the richness of culture, diversity, and appreciation of the finer things in life.

The management of this project also included keeping track of the transportation and delivery of this paraphernalia to Suva. For those conversant with the idiosyncrasies and efficiency of procurement and delivery in India, Fiji had its own peculiar challenges.

Shiro was always house proud, and maintained a beautiful home whether in Delhi or later in Gurgaon. She had been involved with Dastkar, the NGO working with Indian craftsmen to revive the traditional crafts. She had also worked as a coordinator with the film team making Peter Brooks movie based on the epic, the Mahabharata. All that experience came in handy for Shiro.

When India House was finally reopened, it became the talk of the town and Shiro was the consummate hostess who would tell stories of India whilst celebrating the art objects which graced every room. Prof. Mahavir Singh, the Director of the Indian Cultural Centre, persuaded the *Fiji National One* to do a feature on the redone India House, which then spawned a documentary on India House which was shown widely in Fiji and New Zealand. Speaking to Rangeeta Prasad, the documentary maker, of the significance of India House and its belongings and décor, Shiro detailed the finer points of the house's artefacts, such as the ancient brass lamps of Kerala, the bronze statues of Nataraja from Tamil Nadu, the cast iron tribal artefacts of Bastar region and the various other artefacts from Kashmir to Kerala.

Once we settled down in India House, the *Island Life* magazine did an extensive feature on Shiromani in July 2006 with the title "Love Blossomed in Fiji" where she spoke at length about her background and her current role. Relating her own family history, Shiro shared that though her paternal and maternal grandfathers were "girmitiyas" her grandmothers were born in Fiji. Shiro's father had been a cane farmer before he went on to start a business which grew into the Pacific Transport Limited Bus Company, one of the biggest transport services in Fiji.

She spoke about her life in the two countries that she loved - Fiji where she was born and raised and India the homeland of her husband and her ancestors. "I am always busy and life as a diplomat's wife is also fulfilling," she said. She further added, "I feel that I can help to contribute to the government and the NGOs efforts to help the poor people because I have a background in development."

In one of her several interviews, Shiromani recalled that she found it difficult when she first went to India because it was so much bigger than Fiji, the climate was different and it had a large population. But she also found it easy to fall in love with India because the people were friendly and hospitable despite their poverty and hardship.

Her public journey as the wife of the Indian High Commissioner began with an informal tea party organised by her schoolmates from St. Joseph's to welcome her back in her new role. She was thrilled when her school friend Bernadette Ganilau, of the incredibly well-connected Ganilau lineage, told her of the programme.

As the first lady of India House, for the two years we were there, she involved herself in a variety of activities fully utilising her vast network of friends extending all the way back to her childhood. She slipped into the role of a patron with consummate ease. As she said confidently but humbly, "There will be no problem taking up such roles as I was born and grew up in Fiji and know what is involved."

Early in her professional life, Shiro had decided to make working with women a large part of her public persona. Women, in her opinion, were mentally and emotionally strong, partly by nature and by their own experiences. "I think that not enough women realise their strength and I feel that women should recognise it and put it to effective use, "she would often say. "A role that they play instinctively but without realising it is that they are teachers and educators because the home is the first classroom for every child and the first teacher is their mother more than the father."

It was thus that Shiro came to work closely with the NGO, Foundation for Rural Integrated Enterprises "N" Development (FRIEND) for its micro-finance Save scheme to help women gain financial independence. She organised several fund-raising programmes in collaboration with FRIEND. One of those events was at the International Women's Day function at India House where FRIEND members displayed their artwork, their pickles, their jams and all things that traditional family homes value, even as she ensured that business houses were also at hand to help find distributors for their products.

The other significant project she associated herself with was the Makoi Health Centre, a private public partnership in one of the fastest growing areas of the city of Suva. The main people which used the centre were squatters who had had to relocate to the city after their traditional farms had been repossessed by native land-owners.

In Fiji native land holdings are protected and farmers are given fixed term leases. These leases are normally renewed but more recently renewals had not been forthcoming and often three generations who had grown on the farm found themselves dispossessed. So they drifted to the cities for casual work. Hence, the unplanned squatter settlements and the Makoi Health Centre.

Shiromani also started an informal Film Club in which old classics and other Hindi movies were screened. This idea of movie diplomacy was her own and it was well appreciated by the audience which often included Fiji's Vice-President Ratu Joni Madraiwiwi apart from several foreign diplomats.

This idea of the Film Club was initiated during the visit of the eminent Indian Jurist Fali F Nariman and Mrs. Bapsi Nariman whom we hosted at India House in August 2006. As Shiro wrote in an email to Bapsi Nariman, "I really appreciate your offer to get us some old Hindi movies to help start off my film club 'to make friends and influence persons' important for our diplomatic assignment here." On return from her Fiji trip, Bapsi responded through an email where she thanked Shiro immensely for the hospitality and sent a list of 20 classic movies which were available in good condition.

Shiro paid minute attention to the detail and criteria in her selection of movies. She shared her choice of six movies with Bapsi which included; Raj Kapoor's *Shree 420* and *Awara,* and Guru Dutt's *Mrs. and Mr. 55, Kagaz ke Phool and Sahib, Bibi aur Ghulam.* She also wanted a Dev Anand classic. Her choice was either *Paying Guest, Aar Paar or Kala Bazaar.*

Talking about her selection of these six movies she wrote, "We already have a mix of three great actors of the 50s and 60s - Raj Kapoor, Dev Anand and Guru Dutt. It would be good to have a balance of the serious tragedies. I am so thrilled to see that your list includes these and the light hearted romantic comedies such as *Mr. and Mrs. 55* and *Paying Guest* is in the gentle romance genre." The film club increased in popularity and its numbers swelled rapidly.

In addition to her public persona Shiro took personal care of the many problems of the staff of the Mission as the honorary Chairperson of the mission's Ladies Club for the spouses. She was warm and friendly with the junior officers wives, encouraging them to open up and talk freely about their problems and to whom she offered practical advice and support. Shiro was well connected and could deploy assistance easily.

The Indian government offered 25 scholarships to Fiji nationals for studies in India. Before the Fiji High Commission was opened in 2005, Shiro had acted as a guide and guardian to Fiji students in India. Our house in Delhi was an open house for Fiji students. This role of guiding the young students continued after coming to Fiji. Having herself been a student of Delhi University, Shiro was familiar with the challenges of studying in India. She organised counselling sessions at India House, where the young students also met with senior alumni of Indian educational institutions. For many, their bosses had also studied in India on similar scholarships.

Shiromani loved the sea and was very fond of swimming. This was one of the main reasons she was thrilled at my appointment and the prospect of going to Fiji. On the day we landed at Nadi airport, she wanted to dive into the sea as soon as we reached the hotel at Denarau. She told the *Fiji Times* that It was her memories of family picnics at Lami, Wainadoi and Debua beaches that made her long for home. "My father-in-law used to make fun of me when I felt homesick in India, He used to say I was feeling sea sick." When we went on picnic trips with the families of the mission to Deuba beach she would teach the children how to dive and see the corals and treasures of the sea.

One of our more memorable trips was to Taveuni, the third largest Island in the chain of Fiji Islands, which is also known as the Garden Island. Taveuni was one of the confederacies which constituted Fiji at the time of the Deed of Cession to Britain in 1874. Ratu Sir Peaia Ganilau, the last Governor-General of Fiji and its first President was the Tui Cakau of Taveuni, the title tracing his family' lineage as the island's paramount chief. His son, Ratu Epeli Ganilau, was the Minister for Defence and a friend from my younger years.

I happened to mention to Ratu Epeli that I planned to visit Taveuni. After that, everything fell in place to make the trip exceptional. The journey by ship from Savusavu in Vanua Levu to Taveuni is an experience in itself. Ratu Epeli graciously invited us to stay at his beautiful villa located on the seaside. His caretaker there gave us the VIP treatment, not only because we were guests of the family but also because, at Ratu Epeli's advice, I had taken along a bottle of Scotch whisky and a carton of cigarettes for him.

When we visited the Bouma National Heritage Park, Shiro was, predictably, dead keen to go deep into the rain forest to see the tagimoucia flower which is found only in Taveuni. According to Fijian legend, the tagimoucia flower was formed by the tears of a beautiful princess who was in love with a handsome commoner. The father of the princes did not approve of the alliance and the princess fled into the thick rainforest. She lost her way and got exhausted wandering in the woods; she wept for some time and finally fell asleep. Those tears of the princess turned into the tagimoucia flower.

The flower grew only in the higher reaches of the mountain and was difficult to find. When Queen Elizabeth visited Fiji (she was Queen of Fiji till it became a Republic after a coup in 1987 and visited Fiji seven times between her coronation and till it ceased to be a Dominion), she was invariably welcomed with tagimoucia flowers. A team of women from some Taveuni villages would make the difficult climb to pick the flowers for the occasion.

The flower now forms the Fiji emblem, reflecting the special significance and honour it holds for the Fijians.

Shiro was always adventurous, ready to take on any challenge. She insisted on going to see the flower though I tried to point out, weakly, that neither of us were at an age when we could wander around in the forests. But she said that there was another attraction in the Bouma National park; the International Date Line passes through it and one can stand on the 180-degree longitude Meridian and it would be today on the one side and tomorrow on the other. It was another matter that the dateline takes a detour on the map so that the entire Fijian territory falls on one side of the line. But it was not easy to win an argument with Shiromani.

Shiro was my helpmate, ready to give a hand whenever I asked her. But she held her own opinions. She had not witnessed poverty in her upbringing but had a sound theoretical understanding on account of working with the poverty alleviation and developmental programs of the DFID in India. When we returned home, we sometimes had heated discussions on the subject of poverty with our divergent approaches to the issue.

Her real encounter with poverty took place when I contested the Indian Parliamentary election from Agra in 1989. The constituency was vast in area, comprising 8.9 lakh voters; almost equal to the total population of Fiji. She would accompany me in my campaigning, walking into the thatched houses in villages to talk to the women about the problems they faced. It was altogether a new experience to her but she took to campaigning like a duck takes to water. As she told a reporter of the Mumbai daily, *Mid-Day*, "I enjoyed it tremendously. Getting in touch with people of all classes, hearing their problems, helping them out." "It's very satisfying," she concluded in a manner that would do any politician husband proud.

It was my first election, and my friends – school friends, college friends, former colleagues of various hues – academics, lawyers, activists, artists, theatre persons, descended on Agra in droves. Some drove up in their cars, others took the inter-city bus or the convenient early morning train. Shiro looked after all of them, organised their day's activities, sending some of them to see the Taj Mahal and Agra Fort before attending a rally I was addressing that day. Others tried their hand at door-to-door campaigning under close supervision by Shiro or a trusted worker. Journalist friends were given a run down about the constituency and directed to friendly villages.

To one visitor she assigned a well-versed and politically knowledgeable party worker to accompany him for the next few days with a list of villages and other places for them to tour. Clad in a cotton kurta pyjama, the visitor followed me for a whole day of campaigning. He then travelled to the villages and places of significance and took copious notes for a week. He talked to different types of people, from villagers, townsmen and women, the tannery workers and the shoe-makers.

The worker scanned the newspapers and magazines to check what kind of coverage I was getting from this traveller but found nary a word.

Eventually he inquired, "Vikramji, you are not reporting?" Vikram replied he was writing a book and wanted to familiarise himself with the rural life and politics of Uttar Pradesh. My supporter was not amused as he told me agitatedly that evening.

Three years later, best selling author Vikram Seth's magnum opus, "A Suitable Boy" hit the stands to rave reviews. It was a finely crafted and wide spanning saga of society and life in India in the 1950s. Did I see any reflections of Seth's days in Agra in the book? I am not sure. But Shiro thoroughly enjoyed reading the book. Almost two decades later, filmmaker Mira Nair made a six-part TV serial of the book for BBC One, but Shiro was not there to watch it.

My victory in this election-led to a berth in the Union Council of Ministers as Deputy Minister for Railways in Prime Minister V P Singh's government. Shiro was very excited-and had great plans for my constituency. She had noted the demands of the voters wherever she visited them. But the government survived for only one and half years which gave little time for the plans to be implemented.

By the time I again contested the 1996 election from Agra constituency, Shiro had formed her own opinions on Indian politics, so she was able to face media persons with even greater confidence. Talking to *Newspress* she said, "I can tell you when I was campaigning, I saw the conditions in which the people were living and I felt very guilty thinking that here I am asking for their votes when they don't have proper drinking water!" As the correspondent Praveen Talan added, "It was not a political statement of double standards but a genuine heartfelt expression of a compassionate Shiromani Singh who has undauntingly taken the herculean task of campaigning for her husband former union minister Ajay Singh and now a candidate from Janata Dal."

The correspondent further wrote, "Shiromani Singh strikes you as a face of courage, dignity, and quiet strength! She is not put down by the simmering heat or unwanted remarks by some and goes from place to place interacting on a one to one basis with the voters asking them to vote for Ajay Singh; not just on the party policies but for him as an individual as a good person!" Emphasising the point of seeking votes on the basis of my personal qualities, she told the reporter, "He is a character without any blemish, nobody can blame him; he does not have a single charge of corruption against him."

She was aware of the problems of Agra and kept trying to look for ways to sort them out. It was not that she did not face odd questions and situations during electioneering. There was the time when some people complained bitterly about the overflowing sewage and similar problems. She remained unperturbed and calmly pointed out to them that it was the work of the municipal corporation headed by the BJP Mayor. She told them, "I feel very sympathetic but then my husband got hardly one and half year and furthermore only six months as a minister during which he did a lot of work including starting the Inter-city express."

She always said she loved working with people, especially children-related projects even though we didn't have any children.

In 2016, Shiro was diagnosed with breast cancer. Over the next year plus, she was treated by the best specialists in India and abroad. Shiro was brave and strong-willed, determined not to let the illness drag down her spirits. She remained positive in her resolve to fight the cancer. Maneka Gandhi whose mother, Amteshwar, had been a cancer patient, invited us for lunch and advised her to go to Bangalore and try alternative methods of treatment. We did that and also acted on almost all the other suggestions which came our way: Ayurveda, Homeopathy, Yoga, naturopathy et al.

Some friends even suggested that sometimes *duas* (prayers) work, when medicine fails. A friend suggested that she offer a *chader* at the Dargah (Shrine) of Khawaja Moinuddin Chishti at Ajmer. When she found that it was not possible for her to go to Ajmer, she asked me to do this. I visited Ajmer Sharif with a couple of friends.

On the evening I returned, she felt so confident and hopeful and her eyes had their old sparkle. She was to go to the US for further treatment the next day. She went with great expectations and hope. But it was not to be. The specialist at the Stanford hospital clinic told her that the treatment she was getting in India was the best available and advised her to return home to be with her family and friends. This shattered all her hopes.

In Medanta Hospital she would recall her love story and share sweet memories with the attending staff. Two days before her death she had a long chat, rather, a monologue with the duty nurse. The nurse appreciated her courage and cheerfulness and told her, "Ma'm, you are very beautiful, you have lovely eyes, a sweet voice and a very kind heart." Shiro retorted,

"No, no, my husband is also a very tall handsome man, you see him when he comes tomorrow morning."

Next day, the nurse told me that Sir, "Ma'm told me your love story in great detail. She also told me how you proposed to her in the India House in Fiji and promised to take her to a place seven seas away."-

She returned home for the last time. A day after, on November 8, 2017 she was gone. She passed away peacefully, surrounded by her loved ones: her sister, Vijaylakshmi who was her mainstay during her illness, her three brothers, Satya, Vijay and Kishore and her *bhabhi* who flew down from Australia and New Zealand, and my two sisters, including my elder sister, Abha, who flew down from America with her husband, Karan, to be with Shiro in her last days.

That was my "love' Shiromani.

VII

CHAPTER

My Days in Fiji - A Diplomatic Challenge

"This is my play's last scene; here heavens appoint
my pilgrimage's last mile"

John Donne-6th Holy Sonnet

In late December 1976, I brought my Fiji born wife Shiromani Tiwari Singh to my ancestral village, Jaingara. Her own forefathers had gone to Fiji, two generations back, from a village named Dhakaiya in nearby Faizabad District.

The entire village of Jaingara and many more from surrounding areas had gathered at our ancestral home to welcome my *videshi* (foreigner) bride. Our first task was to visit the ancient Dauji Mandir to seek the village deity's blessings. We then entered the ancestral home where the excitedly curious women of the village had thronged the main hall. The men had made themselves comfortable in the verandah and the courtyard under the spreading branches of the old neem tree of the old house. After their first look at Shiromani their surprised exclamation was "*Are yeh to bilkul hamare jaisi hai!*". They were expecting to see the foreigner looking different.

Some 30 years later I went back to my *sasural* (my wife's natal home), the land where my forefathers had first gone 124 years ago. I was returning to the land that had beckoned my great grandparents, my grandfather and then my parents. I was returning as the High Commissioner of a rising Asian power, India. The love story had come full circle.

I took up my assignment as India's High Commissioner to Fiji in March 2005. This was a very emotional occasion for me and Shiromani. After presenting my credentials to the Acting President Ratu Joni Madraiwiwi, Shiromani and I drove in our formal regalia to pay our respects to retired Appeals Court Justice Ghananand Mishra. He was the senior most progeny of Badri Maharaj who in 1890 had helped my great grandmother escape from Penang to Suva.

My appointment to Fiji was a dream come true, but it also brought with it a few challenges. The emotional ties with Fiji notwithstanding, I had a greater responsibility as India's High Commissioner. The Indian government had launched its "Look East" policy with an enhanced focus on the South-east Asian region in the 1990s and was now expanding it further to the east. It was time to give a further thrust to India's relations with Fiji and the South Pacific region. And it was my responsibility to strengthen the ties of friendship and bilateral relations which had suffered after the military coup in 1987.

The nearly 30 years between my father's departure and my arrival had been unusually eventful in Fiji's politics and governance. In the interregnum Fiji had had repeated episodes of an unfortunate sequence — a military coup, a military regime after the coup and then a military controlled interim government followed by democratically elected governments.

The fundamental tension in Fiji's body politic continued to be between ethnic Fijians and Fijians of Indian origin, mainly descendants of "girmitiyas". Between them they comprise 95% of the country's population of around a million with Fiji Indians being marginally greater in number. Indian Fijians, as we have noted, had come to occupy an equal place in the country's society and power structure, to the deep discomfort and disquiet of the ethnic Fijians who believed, with good reason, that this was their land.

Fiji faced its first constitutional crisis in 1977, when the Indo-Fijian dominated National Federation Party (NFP) narrowly won the parliamentary elections. On account of the delay in formation of the government by the winning Indian party, ethnic Fijian Governor General Ratu Sir George Cakobau called on Ratu Sir Kamisese Mara's Fijian Alliance to form a caretaker government, pending new elections scheduled for September of that year. Splits within the NFP and its hesitation to take office also exasperated the situation. In September, Mara's Alliance Party won and took control of the government.

A decade later saw another instance of the inter-racial boil in Fiji coming to surface, this time with fraught consequences. In 1987, Col. Sitiveni Rabuka, a middle level officer, deposed the democratically elected government of Prime Minister Timoci Bavadra. Rabuka believed the government was dominated by Indians even though it was headed by an ethnic Fijian. He later cut the ties with the British crown and declared Fiji a Republic with a President and a new racially discriminatory constitution. This was called the second coup by Rabuka. This was the second constitutional crisis.

The coups caused the exodus of thousands of Indo-Fijians, who faced ethnic discrimination at the hand of the government. In 1990 the interim government promulgated a new Constitution which sought to strengthen ethnic Fijian control of the country. Under this Constitution the positions of President and Prime Minister could only be filled by ethnic Fijians. Thirty-seven of the seventy parliamentary seats could only be filled by ethnic Fijians, giving them a majority in parliament.

In 1992 Rabuka became Prime Minister under the 1990 Constitution. However, he could only do so with the aid of the Indo-Fijian dominated Fiji Labor Party (FLP) and later the National Federation Party (NFP). Expectedly, the FLP and NFP extracted from Rabuka a commitment to carry out the constitutional review which the 1990 constitution had mandated.

In 1995 Rabuka established the Constitutional Review Commission whose report resulted in Fiji's third constitution, the 1997 Constitution. The Constitution undid the discriminatory provisions of the 1990 constitution, resulted in Fiji being re-admitted to the Commonwealth.

The third coup in May 2000 was led by an indigenous Fijian nationalist and failed businessman George Speight who overthrew the first elected government headed by an ethnic Indian on its very first anniversary. In the elections in late 1999, a wide ranging, multiracial People's Coalition led by the Fiji Labour Party won a landslide victory and elected Mahendra Chaudhary as the Prime Minister. Speight held Chaudhary and his senior Cabinet colleagues hostage for 56 days.

The Fiji armed forces under its chief, Josaia Voreqe Bainimarama assumed control and negotiated an end to the two month long standoff and abrogated the Constitution. With the backing of the Great Council of Chiefs, the military installed an interim government headed by Laisenia Qarase, from the nationalist Fiji United Party, an organisation of ethnic Fijians.

Qarase hails from Mavana, a small village of Vanua Balavu of Lau group of Islands and is believed to have native Fijian, Tongan and Jewish ancestry. He studied at Suva Boys Grammar school and graduated in commerce from University of Auckland, He then entered the Fiji civil service, where he served in various ministries and the earned the distinction of being the first ethnic Fijian to be made the managing director of the Fiji Development Bank where he worked for a decade and half. He developed excellent rapport with the Indian business community as well during this period.

He was initially engaged by the interim government as an advisor to prepare a roadmap for the economic development and growth of the Fiji economy but he soon emerged as the consensus choice for the interim Prime Minister of Fiji. Ethnic Fijians dominated this new interim government.

Democratic governance returned to Fiji with elections in 2001 with Qarase as the elected Prime Minister. This was the prevailing governance structure when I landed there four years later.

The first major event under my stewardship was our Independence Day celebrations on August 15, 2005, not at India House but at a hotel. The Independence Day celebration is usually a gala occasion with a heavy participation of the Indian community and Indian expatriates living in Fiji. The function began with unfurling the Indian tri-colour followed by my reading out the address given by the Prime Minister from the rampart of the Red Fort in Delhi.

I then ventured into telling the audience about the inseparable bonds of history, culture and kith ship which were sealed between India and Fiji when the first batch of 498 workers were brought to Fiji in 1879 to provide the much needed human resources for the sugar industry. My own inseparable bond was forged soon afterwards when my paternal great grandparents arrived at Nukulau Island in 1885. I said this with a sense of humility as I am the fourth-generation of my family to form this indelible part of our shared history with Fiji.

My story was a pleasant surprise to the many who were not familiar with it and it was so refreshing for those in the audience who knew a little bit about it. There was much excited comment from many Fijians and diplomats of other countries, while a few of the descendants of the "girmitiyas" claimed I was like one of them. The function had a striking effect on both the Fijian and Indian guests and later became the talk of the town.

As it happens, I was also born on August 15 and over the years I have created a punch line for occasions when I am asked my date of birth. It goes something like this: "It is the day celebrated by over 1.25 billion people." I have received some very confused, surprised or amused responses to that one.

Perhaps the proudest birthday I celebrated was the next year when Shiromani and I hosted the Independence day celebrations on the sprawling lawns of the newly refurbished India House. Here was I the official representative of the Government of India hosting independent India's birthday, in the historical official residence of the Indian High Commissioner!

The Indian mission in Suva had been shut down in the aftermath of the military coup in Fiji in 1987 as had the Indian Cultural Centre. The High Commission was reopened in March 1999 after more than a decade, but the Indian Cultural Centre had not been restored in this time. The residents of Suva missed the Cultural Centre. The Indian community took great pride in the display of Indian culture by the performances of the artistes, and there was an often voiced demand in Suva for reopening the Culture centre and resuming the cultural activities. The Girmit Centre at Lautoka had taken over the responsibility of looking after the ICCR Scholarship schemes in the absence of the Mission and the ICC.

Senior leaders and prominent Indians had also sought the reopening of the Centre. Former Prime Minister Mahendra Chaudhary during his visits to India had raised the issue at several meetings with the ICCR and MEA. I too, as High Commissioner designate, took up the matter vigorously with the Ministry and the ICCR and asked for the immediate reopening of the ICC on a larger scale than before.

I was aware of the significance of the Cultural Centre for the Indian community in Fiji and its role in Indian diplomacy in the region. The proposal for reopening the Cultural Centre in Fiji had been making the rounds in official files for some time without a decision, but my forceful push for its immediate reopening had an effect. The proposal was approved and things started moving fast. I was still in Delhi and kept pressing various officials to ensure an early start to the Cultural Centre. The approval for posting two Indian artistes also came through and an accomplished Kathak dancer and a tabla player were appointed on the condition that they moved to Suva immediately. Later a Yoga teacher was also sent to Suva.

It was thus that the Indian Cultural Centre was reopened in Suva in February 2005, even before I got there. The two artistes, Kathak Dancer Vidha Lal and Tabla Artiste Rajiv Shukla soon arrived in Suva. We were fortunate to get two other artistes in bonus as spouses of the official appointees. Vidha's husband Abhimanyu and Rajiv's wife Surabhi, both excellent Kathak dancers, accompanied their spouses. On certain important occasions all four performed together and made an impressive team. They drew a large number of students and others for their classes.

As the Indian Cultural Centre became a part of Suva's cultural scene, there grew a strong demand in Fiji's western region, the heartland of the Indian settlement, for a sub-centre of the Cultural Centre to be established in Lautoka town. I strongly supported the demand and wrote to the Ministry and ICCR backing the proposal.

As a result of my robust advocacy, the Director-General of the ICCR Surya Kanti Tripathi made a visit to Fiji to assess the viability of the demand. The proposal was approved and a sub-centre of the Cultural Centre was established at the Girmit Centre in Lautoka town in the heart of the cane-growing region of Fiji. The Yoga teacher was posted to the sub-centre in Lautoka. The ICC Sub-Centre was inaugurated by Sri Somnath Chatterjee, Speaker of the Lok Sabha who was visiting Fiji for a Commonwealth conference, in September 2005.

The inaugural function of the ICC sub-centre was attended by the Vice-President of Fiji, Ratu Joni Madraiwiwi, the Prime Minister Laisenia Qarase, former Prime Minister Mahendra Chaudhary, and Y. P. Reddy, Chairman of the Girmit Centre. The Girmit Centre in Lautoka had been inaugurated by Indian Prime Minister Indira Gandhi during the historic first ever visit by an Indian Prime Minister to Fiji in 1981 and had become the centre of Indian cultural activities in the Western Region. The ICC Sub-Centre Lautoka was located within the Girmit Centre campus. The inauguration was followed by a scintillating performance by the ICC artistes, which was witnessed by a large audience.

Sometime later Prof. Mahavir Singh, a senior academic who had held distinguished positions in the government of India under the Ministry of Culture, was appointed as Director of the Indian Cultural Centre. With his arrival in Suva in January 2006, the Centre's activities acquired a new momentum. Professor Singh planned and designed a refurbished Indian Cultural Centre which was inaugurated by Vayalar Ravi, Minister for Overseas Indian Affairs, in October 2006. Mahavir Singh's innovative ideas and long experience as a Cultural and Educational administrator soon made the Centre a hub of cultural and creative activity in Suva.

Life in Suva settled into the usual diplomatic whirl of calling on ministers and other dignitaries, attending public events, lectures, official functions and other mundane routine of official work. I travelled across the main island of Viti Levu, visiting Lautoka, Ba and the smaller towns in the sugarcane region. This included Rakiraki, a town with which our family has had a relationship since 1885 and where my grandfather was born.

An important port of call was Labasa town on the other main island, Vanua Levu, I made several trips to Labasa during my tenure. Labasa was one of the earliest places where girmityas had settled. It once had a flourishing sugar industry with the Labasa sugar mill being one of the most productive.

In later years Labasa developed another distinction: of producing many of Fiji's most successful intellectuals. Prominent academics, lawyers, doctors, politicians, administrators and educationists who have served Fiji over the years are proud Labasans. Among the most famous Labasans currently is footballer Roy Krishna, the goal scoring phenomenon who is the captain of ATK Mohun Bagan in the Indian Super league and of the Fiji National team. Brij Lal, the prominent Fiji-born Australian historian and academic, has written widely about his "girmit" heritage and the struggles of his family in Labasa.

Well before starting my journey to Fiji, I was quite clear about the situation there, what my agenda should be and the challenges to be faced. The issues had been in my mind and I had often articulated them on different occasions and at meetings for some time. I had strongly advocated that as the term 'Indo-Pacific' was gaining currency in the global strategic and political discourse, India should take a closer look at the South Pacific region. This region stretched across the Central and Eastern Indo-Pacific.

The region had long been of interest to India due to the presence of a large minority of people of Indian origin in Fiji. In the early 1900s it was the plight of the "girmitiyas" which drove Gokhale and Gandhi to lead the fight to abolish the indentured labour system in 1916. In addition there were linkages with the island nations through the Commonwealth. The political instability in Fiji had reduced interaction with the region for long periods. The goodwill for India in the region had declined in the past decades because of a perceived Indian disinterest. This had to be rebuilt and nurtured with positive engagement. The Pacific Islands Forum (PIF), comprising 14 island states with India as a Dialogue Partner, was a suitable vehicle for reaching out to the island states.

Regional forces had long cast their own shadow and new forces were emerging. Fiji's traditional supporters, Australia and New Zealand, had enhanced their interaction with the PIF but had been very critical of political developments in Fiji since the first coup in 1987. Their stance was unfriendly and their criticisms had a patronising tone which was offensive to the leadership in Fiji. An expansionist China on the other hand was prepared to fill the breach and did so. It had visually stepped up its engagement in the region with liberal loans for infrastructure projects. The Chinese influence was bound to grow.

India's main asset was the deep cultural ties with the Indian diaspora and the disapora's ripple effects through the society they settled into. Indian cuisine, culture, dress, music, dance, drama has permeated throughout Fiji. Indian cuisine is affordable and enjoyable. Most Fijian homes, be they in traditional Fijian villages, or towns and cities, with mixed ethnicities families, enjoy their roti and curry. Samosas and *bhajiyas* are favoured fast foods. Bollywood also has made inroads and many households organise their day around the timing of the latest serials. The current government's recognition of all citizens as Fijians regardless of their ancestry had been a welcome development.

This soft diplomacy has been nurtured over the years and my father Bhagwan Singh, the first Indian High Commissioner to the newly independent Fiji, promoted this by opening his and his family's heart to the country of his father's birth. India House was open and welcoming. Indeed India was open and welcoming to students, visitors, pilgrims and those with an interest in the arts and culture.

A powerful bond was religion. In every town there was a mandir, a mosque, and schools managed by the Arya Samaj, the Sanatan Pratinidhi

Sabha or an Islamic Association, Sangam or a Sikh Organisation. Festivals of all Indian religions were celebrated with gusto. The Indian Government needed to build on this base.

The Indian government had some schemes to provide scholarships and training programmes for Fiji such as the Indian Technical and Economic Cooperation (ITEC), general cultural scholarships, Hindi training and Colombo Plan. These programmes are popular with students and are an effective means of public outreach for India in many developing countries.

I began work on increasing the number of slots allotted to Fiji under these schemes. At the same time I made efforts to revive the Alumni Association of Fijians who had studied in India; this was a pool of goodwill for India and I was keen to make it an active association creating awareness of Indian capabilities.

Another early initiative was to boost the Hindi teaching programme through collaboration with the Department of Education and the Hindi Teachers' Association of Fiji. The Hindi teaching programme was meant to encourage reading and writing in Hindi.

Indians in Fiji have retained their ancestral language; they speak a form of Hindi which is called Fiji *baat* or Fiji Hindi. Traditionalist Hindi partisans looked down on Fiji Hindi but respect for Fiji Hindi shot up after Prof. Subramani, prominent Indo-Fijian academic and writer, began to write in Fiji Hindi in the early 2000s. His first book 'Dauka Puran' was acclaimed even in India and his second book 'Fiji Maa' was also well received.

Fiji has numerous Indian social organisations, bhajan mandalis and other sangathans. Under a government scheme we distributed musical instruments and books, especially the Indian epics and other literature.

The first year of my tenure was hectic with two major events, the Commonwealth Parliamentarians' Association (CPA) conference in September and the visit of Fiji's Prime Minister to India in October. My first major challenge in Fiji was the 51st conference of the Commonwealth Parliamentarians Association.

The conference, which is held once in three years, took place in Nadi from 1st to 9th September 2005 and was attended by Speakers and Parliamentarians from all Commonwealth Countries. Nadi town on the western side of Viti Levu, was chosen as the venue of the conference as the international airport is nearby and it is easily accessible to a string of high end hotels and island resorts in the vicinity.

The Indian contingent was the largest of all, comprising speakers from all state assemblies and ten prominent members of parliament. Sushma Swaraj was one of the better known parliamentarians as also Mr. Reshang Keishing of Manipur, the oldest parliamentarian of the country. The delegation was led by Lok Sabha Speaker Somnath Chatterjee. Most leaders were accompanied by their spouses and family members besides the usual team of personal staff. Denarau Island across from Nadi had a cluster of five-star hotels including the Sheraton and all official delegates were lodged there.

I moved across to Nadi together with Anil Anand, my HOC, and Arun Sarkar, Consular Officer and a team of my staff and set up a camp office to deal with the high profile guests. The conference was expected to be a smooth affair but turned out to be one of my most challenging occasions in Fiji.

Shiromani, my staff and I had geared up to host the delegation and their entourage. Many of them had made long, tedious journeys with inter changes of flights enroute. They were exhausted by the time they arrived at Nadi airport. The very first complication cropped up as soon as the first group of delegates landed in Nadi.

The veteran woman politician and speaker from Rajasthan assembly, Mrs. Sumitra Singh, looked visibly upset on arrival. As I greeted her, she angrily told me that her checked in suitcase was missing. Her suitcase had not been loaded on the plane and had instead reached New York. All her clothing was in the suitcase and she had no change of clothing for the inaugural ceremony the next morning. I tried to calm down Sumitraji whom I knew well as a veteran Rajasthan politician but she remained decidedly put off by the missing suitcase.

Shiro then intervened to offer a choice of any sarees from her collection till the missing luggage arrived. Sumitraji retorted that she could borrow a saree, but how would she find a blouse that fitted her to go with the saree. But Shiro was up to the task and assured her that a matching blouse would be ready by early morning.

Through her legion of contacts, Shiro found a woman who came to the hotel, took the measurements and brought back the newly stitched blouse in the morning. Sumitraji was all smiles when she reached the venue of the conference and full of praise for Shiromani. I gave a sigh of relief and mentally thanked my enterprising wife. One disaster averted.

The conference continued and my staff was on their toes. Even the wives of the officers of the mission did their bit in looking after the guests. But the bigger challenge was unfolding at the Conference.

The Conference was to elect a new Chairperson and India had nominated West Bengal Speaker, Hashim Abdul Halim, for the election. It was expected to be a simple election as Halim was a highly respected Speaker, said to be the longest serving Speaker of a legislature in the world. But another candidate emerged who showed signs of giving a good fight. Cook Islands fielded Geoffrey Henry, a former Prime Minister of the country. Being a local candidate from the region and a well regarded politician with close ties in the other island nations, it threatened to become a close contest.

Somnath Chatterjee, the team of senior Indian officials accompanying him and myself plunged into the contest, trying to tie up votes for our candidate. It was a matter of prestige; India had announced its candidate and as a leading member of the Commonwealth anything less than a clear victory would be a loss of face. Also, Hashim Abdul Halim was Speaker of West Bengal Assembly, Somnath Chatterjee's home state and a long standing political colleague. Somnath Chatterjee had led Halim's global campaign for the last six months and Somnathda was also in the contest for Vice President of the CPA.

Even as all the other activities of the Conference went on and the demands and special requests of various delegates were taken care of by my staff, we were busy with the contest. Meetings, impromptu discussions, button-holing people in the lounge and corridors continued. There was a sense of excitement and strong solidarity among the Pacific Islanders over their regional candidate. They had lobbied vigorously with the other small island nations as well as their allies among the western countries.

Voting took place on the concluding day of the conference. As it happened, Halim's victory was facile: he had 188 votes against Henry's 73 votes. It was a handsome victory as Somnath Chatterjee was also elected as Vice President. It was a most satisfactory end to the Conference.

I was touched and immensely gratified to receive a letter from Somnath Ji shortly after he returned to Delhi. Dated 13th September 2005, the letter said: "I wish to record my deepest appreciation of the wonderful arrangements that you made during our stay at Nadi. Our participation in the conference was successful primarily due to the efforts and the initiatives that you took. I am very happy and proud that India is so well represented in Fiji where a lot of problems are being faced by Indians.

"Please accept my sincerest compliments for all the help and assistance that we received. The attention that was given by the High Commission staff under your leadership was exemplary and that enabled us to discharge our functions smoothly and efficiently. Please convey our thanks to Mrs. and Mr. Sarkar for all their kind attention.

"My wife joins me in conveying our sincerest thanks to your gracious wife for all the kind affection that both of us received from her. We shall remember our stay in Nadi for a long time. I wish to convey our personal high regards and our best wishes to both of you. I am convinced that the interests of our country as well as of Indians there are very safe in your hands."

He added that he would be speaking to Minister Natwar Singh about the "wonderful contributions you made for our successful participation at the CPA conference." Somnathji did exactly that: he not only spoke to the minister but also wrote to him.

A few days later, Secretary (East) in the MEA, Rajiv Sikri sent me extracts from his letter to the Minister. The extract read: "I wish to record our highest appreciation of the help and cooperation that Indian delegation received from Shri Ajay Singh, our High Commissioner in Fiji during our stay at Nadi in Fiji. Both the Acting President and the Prime Minister of Fiji had taken the trouble of meeting me in the hotel where we were staying. I believe those meetings at the high level were possible only at the personal initiatives of our High Commissioner. I shall be failing in my duty if I don't record my appreciation of the help that we received from our High Commissioner and his staff."

The Conference was a resounding success for India and Somnathji had been gracious in acknowledging my contribution. I sent him a short letter thanking him for his kind words.

I had very little time to bask in the satisfaction of a successful conference as we immediately plunged into tying up the final arrangements for Prime Minister Laisenia Qarase's official visit to India. Prime ministerial visits are the high points of diplomatic life, bringing to fruition bilateral agreements as well as tightening the bonds of friendship.

I had already made a rushed visit to Delhi in August for consultations. There were a series of back-to-back meetings in South Block, and other government departments and ministries for planning and making arrangements for the visit. The Fiji PM's visit was a very significant one. It was the first ever Prime Ministerial visit with a 70-member delegation which included government officials, members of the Trade and Investment Mission as well as a large contingent of business leaders of Fiji.

I returned to Suva with the satisfaction of having persuaded our foreign office to accord full hospitality to the entire delegation from 8th to 15th October. It was an unusual gesture and was an indication of the high significance being accorded to the visit and the ties with Fiji. India's ties with Fiji had seen its ups and downs with the bouts of political instability in Fiji. The visit aimed to take the bilateral ties to a new level of cooperation.

As a measure of the deepening ties, Fiji was also elevating ties by establishing its first High Commission in New Delhi and the mission was to be inaugurated by Prime Minister Qarase.

The Government of India made splendid arrangements for the visit. Shiromani and I accompanied Prime Minister Qarase and his wife Leba Qarase through his India tour. The visit began with the formal welcome ceremony in the spectacular setting of the forecourt of Rashtrapati Bhawan. Qarase had a fruitful meeting with Prime Minister Manmohan Singh at Hyderabad House, the stately building used for meeting and entertaining high dignitaries. Four Memoranda of Understanding were signed for health, trade and tourism.

After the official part of the visit was completed, the Fijian party travelled to different cities. The Indian government provided a well-appointed aircraft to fly the delegation to Agra for a visit to the Taj Mahal and Fatehpur Sikri. At the Taj Mahal, Qarase recounted his impressions to the correspondent of the *Fiji Daily Post* that the visit was memorable for the Qarases as they had taken the opportunity to reaffirm their love for each other. "It makes you feel love and makes you reaffirm your love," he said.

The delegation then flew to Kochi and Alappuzha in Kerala, and from there to Bangalore and then to Mumbai. They had official engagements at all these places. A good deal of planning had gone into charting the PM's itinerary and the places he would visit. Aside from meetings with the Governors of Maharashtra and Karnataka, discussions with trade organisations, corporate leaders, Qarase also met film producers and directors in Mumbai. The Fiji government was keen to market its beautiful islands as an attractive destination for shooting Indian films.

Visits to the Coir Board, Spice Board, Coconut Development Board in Kerala and Foam matting India Limited in Alappuzha were particularly educative. Fiji is a copra producer and the PM's party were excited to see the variety of products made of coconut trees. A visit to the Bannari Amman Sugar Mill in Mysore impressed Qarase the most. He described it "a modern, integrated and high performing facility," producing raw and refined sugar, also generating electricity and manufactured ethanol and organic fertilizers.

In Bengaluru, the Fiji party visited the Infosys and Biocon facilities. Some businessmen members of the delegation stayed back and held business discussions with counterparts in Ahmedabad and Kolkata. Others made a quick trip to religious places such as Haridwar, Rishikesh and Varanasi.

Prime ministerial visits are high points in the bilateral relations of two countries. The tour was an eye opener for many of the delegates. Most of them had a vague idea about India, mainly gleaned from the western media. What the visitors saw was a thriving democracy with a modern, diversified economy that was among the fastest growing economies in the world. The tour showed them the variety of areas for cooperation. Some delegates returned to Fiji with plans for joint ventures and trade proposals.

The highlight of Qarase's visit was the speech he made at the opening of the Fiji High Commission in Delhi. In a frank and lucid speech, Qarase touched on several issues of concern. Aside from its flattering reference to me and Shiromani, it was a significant address that spoke of ties with India while touching on sensitive issues of racial relations even as it highlighted the lives and contributions of the Indian community in Fiji.

Due to its significance to Fiji-India relations and racial relations in Fiji, I have reproduced the speech below:

> "I bring very cordial greetings to the government and the people of India from the government and people of Fiji. I thank India very much for its invitation to me to make an official visit to coincide with the opening of our High Commission in Delhi.
>
> The members of our delegation from government and the private sector are looking forward very much to learning more about India, its rise on the world stage and the unleashing of its economic potential.

This occasion closes a circle of history, while giving new strength and vitality to the long relationship between India and Fiji.

One hundred and twenty six years ago, pioneers from India crossed the kala pani, the black waters, to become indentured workers in Fiji's sugar industry. They ventured bravely into the unknown, driven by those universal hopes and dreams of humanity for greater opportunities and a better life.

Other people from the sub-continent followed. Conditions on the sugar plantations were hard and often cruel.

When their indentured service finished, around 40,000 of these workers chose to remain and build a future in what was then a British colony. They were joined by more immigrants from India.

The cane fields and sugar mills flourished and were the main pillars of the economy. Indians became independent farmers, central to the sugar industry's success.

As time passed, and the population increased, many went into business, the professions and industry. They constructed schools and places of worship and preserved their culture and traditions.

And so the character and image of Fiji was profoundly transformed.

The Indians shared our Islands with the indigenous Fijians, of Melanesians and Polynesian heritage. There were also minority groups of many origins.

All these peoples, with their different customs, beliefs and values, contributed to Fiji's development.

When Mrs. Indira Gandhi made a memorable visit to our country in 1981, she made the point that wherever Indians had gone, they had enriched their new homelands by their hard work and enterprise. That can certainly be said of our Fiji Indian citizens.

Today, the people of our multicultural society enjoy equal rights under a constitution which calls us to live in harmony and unity. It commits us to promoting social justice, and the economic and social advancement of all communities.

There is a reaffirmation of fundamental freedoms, adherence to the rule of law and respect for human dignity.

The vision of the government I lead is to create a sense of unified nationhood, founded on respect and mutual understanding. We are very much focussed on the reconciling of our society, following civil and political disorder in 2000.

During the time of colonialism, India maintained a diplomatic presence in Fiji. When we became independent in 1970, formal relationships were established by our sovereign states.

Fiji opened a number of missions to represent its international interests. But it was only laterally that we made the decision to open a diplomatic office in Delhi. This was in response to a changing world environment and India's emergence as a new economic and diplomatic force.

We were also beginning to actively expand our bilateral links.

The most significant aspect of this was India's ready willingness to offer help for the reform of our sugar industry.

And so the circle closes.

We are taking our diplomatic relations to higher levels, after all these years, and India has a key position in modernising the very enterprise which created the first bonds between us.

Both our nations are now ready to cross the threshold of a fresh era of cooperation and friendship.

We have always seen India as a world leader and a voice for developing countries.

India provided leadership for the awakening of many former colonies. There was an inevitability about this, given India's size, location and its long struggle for freedom.

It stood at the forefront of non-alignment during the cold war, and was instrumental in reshaping and virtual rebirth of the commonwealth.

India is renowned for the vigour of its democratic system of governance and the cherishing and promotion of democratic ideals.

Pandit Nehru said India could not avoid the various responsibilities arising out of its geography and history.

It's the same today. Many smaller states depend on India to articulate their common concerns with strength and sympathy in the international community.

The smaller countries must, of course, speak out for themselves - and they do. But when India puts its weight and power behind them in organisations like the World Trade Organisation and the United Nations, that makes a substantial difference.

We are glad, therefore, to give our support for India's membership of the UN Security Council. It will make the council more representative and reflect the current geopolitical realities.

We have watched with keen interest as India has reorganised its economy to achieve higher growth. Some of the first steps towards reform were taken when Dr. Manmohan Singh was Finance Minister. As India's Prime Minister, he is guiding the country along the same path of progress. We admire him for his ability and skill.

When I met with the Prime Minister last evening, we discussed some of the critical issues of competitiveness, productivity and investment that apply in the globalised market.

At home we have accomplished our own economic resurgence since 2000. It created a period of unprecedented growth. Our economic fundamentals are firm, we have low inflation, adequate foreign reserves and moderate debt. Investment has increased substantially.

Some of your parliamentarians had a chance to observe what we have done, when they attended a recent meeting in Fiji of the Commonwealth Parliamentary Association. In fact the speaker of your Lok Sabha spoke highly of what we have achieved. We thank him for his compliments.

We anticipate that the fashioning of closer links between our countries will give momentum to our push to increase prosperity for the people of Fiji. There will also be advantages for India.

We have identified numerous opportunities for increased trade, investment and technical cooperation.

We hope to gain access to India's knowledge, expertise and technology in many fields.

The sugar technical mission currently assisting with our sugar industry reform is an example of this. We are extremely grateful for the mission's efforts and for a loan from the government of India through the Exim Bank, for the upgrading of our sugar mills. Indian companies will win new business in supply of equipment.

Yesterday, I co-signed a memorandum of understanding with your Prime Minister that sets out main areas of development co-operation. Included in these are civil aviation, tourism, agriculture, fisheries and forests, sports, cultural exchanges, assistance for small and medium enterprises and specialist training in trade negotiations and diplomacy.

Additionally, there are agreements covering sundry health issues, information communication technology and film production.

Ladies and gentlemen, I have mentioned the importance to Fiji of the setting up of this diplomatic mission. It is one of the government's most significant foreign policy initiatives.

The potential we see is shared by Fiji's private sector. That is why our government delegation is accompanied by the largest contingent of business people ever to join in a visit of this kind. With us are representatives of Fiji's largest and most important companies, all alert to the prospects of trade and investment.

Among them are descendants of those who sailed across black waters so long ago. The dreams of their forebears were not easily accomplished. There was much sacrifice and struggle.

> Now, though, what they hoped for has been realised in full measure. We see that today in the names and the achievements of those who are travelling with us. They are leading citizens of Fiji, whose enterprises are household names. Their contribution to our country and economy is outstanding.
>
> Much effort has gone into preparing for this day and for the new era in India Fiji relations. I offer sincere thanks to the officials from both governments who have done the groundwork and to our High Commissioner, H. E. Mr. Luke Rokovada and his staff for their efforts.
>
> We particularly appreciate the role of India's High Commissioner in Fiji H.E. Mr. Ajay Singh. Ajay brings to his job a deep understanding of Fiji and its people. His father was a former High Commissioner to Fiji and his paternal great grandparents were among the arrivals from India at the end of 19th century.
>
> He is married to a local girl, Shiromani, whose family can also be listed in the roll of honours of our leading citizens and community leaders. Before they left India to take up their diplomatic posting, Shiromani had to make a very important choice. She had to give up her Fiji Passport. It was, I understand, a very emotional decision for her. It was like giving up the part of her that was Fiji, to become a full part of India.
>
> In a very personal sense Ajay and Shiromani represent what is unique and special about Fiji's and India's relationship with each other. Through our common history and cultural connections, we have bonds that are enduring and permanent. In other words, we are forever and irrevocably part of one another.
>
> Ladies and gentlemen, it just remains for me to thank the government of India most sincerely for its financial support for the establishment of the Mission. And let me make this pledge for Fiji, through our High Commission here, we commit ourselves to building with India and its people the closest degree of friendship and cooperation.
>
> I now have much pleasure in declaring Fiji's first High Commission in New Delhi officially open.
>
> *Vinaka vakalevu, bahut dhanyawad*, and thank you for being with us.

The visit was a resounding success. Prime Minister Qarase and his delegation were deeply impressed and gratified by their visit to India. On his return to Suva, Qarase addressed the nation in a national broadcast to speak about his Indian tour. He said that he had briefed Prime Minister Manmohan Singh on the initiative his government had taken to promote reconciliation and unity through legislation. He also explained his proposal to resolve the long standing issue of land leases with secure 50 year leases, with guaranteed number of extensions. He ended his speech by saying: “Everywhere we went there was enormous goodwill for Fiji. It was a heart-warming experience.”

The visit did indeed open up new and varied avenues of cooperation between the two countries. But the visit had not been without its challenges and obstacles. The visit was taking place in the midst of a raging political controversy in Fiji. Qarase had introduced a bill in Parliament titled Promotion of Reconciliation, Tolerance and Unity Bill (PRTUB) which was strongly criticised by some opposition parties, particularly the leader of the Opposition, former Prime Minister Mahendra Chaudhary.

One of the main points of contention was the provision in the bill that allowed for the grant of amnesty to some of the leaders of the 2000 coup who had already been convicted by the courts. Qarase claimed that his reconciliation initiative had drawn from Nelson Mandela’s reconciliation movement in post-apartheid South Africa but the bill had become a matter of intense debate. Opinion within the Fiji Indian community was divided; as it has almost always been on issues of Indian concern.

Barely weeks before the visit, Sam Rajappa, a veteran Indian journalist wrote an article in an Indian newspaper titled ‘Doomed Democracy’ which created a stir in official circles in Suva. Rajappa wrote: “Qarase’s visit to India is ostensibly to declare open the Fiji High Commission in New Delhi. His real purpose is to sooth India’s ruffled feelings about the patently anti-Indian administration he has been running for the last five years.”

He also added that “Anticipating Qarase’s perfidy, (Mahendra) Chaudhary paid a quick visit to New Delhi in September, to brief the PMO and the External affairs Ministry about the real purpose of the large Fiji delegation. The mandarins in the South Block reportedly assured Chaudhary that Prime Minister Manmohan Singh will convey to Qarase India’s unhappiness about the most controversial legislation intended to sideline the Indo-Fijian community.”

Chaudhary had paid a visit to India and as usual had met Indian leaders and opinion makers. Antar Rashtriya Sahyog Parishad, a leading social organisation that promoted cooperation with the Indian diaspora and was headed by my father in the 1960s, organised a seminar on the proposed Promotion of Reconciliation, Tolerance and Unity Bill. Mahendra Chaudhary was the key speaker at the seminar held at Delhi’s Constitution Club.

The ARSP's bulletin edited by its General Secretary, Baleshwar Agrawal carried a report on the seminar, noting: "The Bill is a contentious one and has generated much debate in Fiji and abroad. It contains provisions of granting amnesty to the people who staged a coup in Fiji in 2000 when George Speight stormed into Fiji Parliament with armed gunmen and took hostage the then Prime Minister Mahendra Chaudhary and his ministers. Mahendra Chaudhary dismissed the Fiji government's view that the bill sought to promote reconciliation and tolerance between the two ethnic groups in Fiji. Terming it a farce, he expressed the hope that the Indian government would be able to prevail over Qarase during his October visit to withdraw the bill."

These reports created some disquiet in Suva. I had to do some urgent damage control. I explained that in India, everyone was free to voice their opinion and the Indian media was often caustic. I said that the reports did not reflect the view of the government of India and a warm welcome awaited Prime Minister Qarase in Delhi.

To the External Affairs Ministry senior officials in Delhi, I pointed out that the controversy was about a draft bill that had still to go through Parliament and was being vigorously debated in the country. It was the opportune time to give a new thrust to Fiji-India relations; the visit went ahead as planned.

On his return to Fiji, Prime Minister Qarase wrote a letter to me conveying his thanks for the excellent arrangements made for their visit. The visit, he wrote, was a real eye opener for all of us from Fiji. "We returned from India fully convinced that there is much Fiji can learn from India."

Qarase also made special mention of Shiro and her efforts made in looking after the Fiji students in Delhi. "On a personal note, I was deeply moved to hear from the Fiji students studying in India of how Shiromani was such a wonderful 'mother' to them in always freely availing herself to provide assistance and guidance. This was before the establishment of the Fiji High Commission, and all I can say is; *vinaka vakalevu.*" (thank you very much). He also wrote separate letters to the President APJ Abdul Kalam and Prime Minister Manmohan Singh for their generosity in receiving and welcoming them.

Shortly afterward, I received a letter from Minister K. Natwar Singh, dated October 31, 2005 which said: "Dear Ajay, My attention has been drawn to the remarks made by the Prime Minister of Fiji, Mr. Laisenia

Qarase, at the official opening of the Fiji High Commission in New Delhi on October 11, 2005. I was glad to see the very laudatory references he made to you and Shiromani and to the tremendous contributions that you are making to India-Fiji relations. You are doing a superb job. Please keep it up." My cup brimmed over!

The new year saw the unfurling of the Indian Flag after many years at India House. for the Republic Day celebrations on 26th January. India House had been restored and we had moved in even though the furniture that we had ordered from India was yet to arrive. There was a quiet sense of joy among the Indians present at the sight of the tricolour fluttering in the mild breeze of a sunny Suva morning. The iconic building was a cherished landmark for the Indian community in Suva. A few hundred people attended the event where the address to the nation by President Abdul Kalam was read out.

A formal reception was held later in the evening which was attended by Prime Minister Qarase and Mrs. Leba Qarase and several Cabinet members. Other guests included Chief Justice Daniel Fatiaki and Mrs. Martha Fatiaki, Speaker of the House of Representatives Ratu Epeli Nailatikau and Adi Koila Nailatikau, President of the Senate, Taito Waqavakatoga, and Mrs. Makreta Waqavakatoga, leader of opposition Mahendra Chaudhary and Mrs. Veermati Chaudhary. The chief guest on the occasion was the Vice-President, Ratu Joni Madraiwiwi.

Our national day reception was unlike any other in Fiji since we did not serve alcoholic drinks at the Republic Day reception according to Indian tradition. The joke in the diplomatic community was that the Indians had the most well attended reception despite not serving liquor – a most unusual practice in Fiji where social drinking, occasionally even heavy drinking was the norm.

There is a trace of informality in Fijian life and I used to receive a number of visitors at my office. One fine morning, a small group of Gujarati businessmen were chatting with me, when one of them remarked that it would soon be a hundred years since the first Gujarati merchants arrived in Fiji. It struck me that it would be a good idea to mark the occasion with a public function. I immediately suggested to my friends, Bachu Bhai, Hari Punja, Ajay Amrit et al that the event deserves celebration. They picked the idea at once and went on to discuss the proposal with the office bearers of the Fiji Gujarat Samaj.

The samaj was very enthusiastic and they immediately called meetings, raised funds and chalked out an elaborate year-long programme of celebrations. The centenary programme began with a *hawan* on the 1st April 2006 in Lautoka while the formal inaugural program was held on 2nd April. I was invited as the chief guest for the inaugural. There were more than 3000 people at the function housed in an air conditioned tent erected on the lawns of Lautoka park. People came from all over Fiji, and some of them even came from overseas – Gujaratis who had moved from Fiji to Australia and New Zealand and on to some of the smaller islands. The formal inauguration was followed by cultural programmes, Bollywood dance performances by the ladies, children and people of Gujarati community. It was a whole day event with a festive atmosphere.

The organising committee also brought out a souvenir which carried articles on the prominent and pioneering Gujarati families and their early lives in Fiji. It also had messages from leaders of the government, politicians and other prominent citizens. Different activities were organised throughout the year from April 2006 to 2007 culminating in a concluding function held in Suva.

The concluding session of the Gujarati Centenary celebrations was held in the FMF Dome in Suva in April 2007 which had a capacity of about 5,000 people. The invitees included the who's who of Fiji. Right from the Prime Minister who was the Chief Guest to almost all senior government functionaries, the Diplomatic corps and a goodly section of the Gujarati community in Suva.

The Gujarati audience was quite pleased with Prime Minister Qarase's speech as he highlighted the contribution of the Gujarati community in nation building and development of Fiji. I was given the honour to address the gathering before the Prime Minister spoke. My short speech which focused on the community's contribution to the economic growth of Fiji from a mere sugar exporter to a more diverse economy, was well received.

A Gujarati Garba Dandiya troupe from the Nataraj Kala Mandir of Rajkot was sent to Fiji by the ICCR to tour Fiji for the occasion. The Garba troupe performed at the concluding function to the delight of the Gujarati audience, followed by a performance by the artists of our Cultural Centre.

The ICCR had also sent Bhai Chand Patel as their representative. Bhai Chand, a Fiji -born international diplomat, is based in Delhi where he served as United Nations Regional Director. Bhai Chand is well-known in Delhi's social circles for his parties and irreverent writings in the daily papers.

He made an emotional speech, saying that he carried both Fiji and India within him. He then pulled out the blue Fiji Passport from his pocket and said that though he had lived outside Fiji for the last 35 years, he still retained his blue book. He said he was a product of India because when he left Fiji in 1956 for studies in India, there were not many opportunities for higher education at home or abroad.

He very emphatically said with a touch of gratitude, "if the government of India had not given me the scholarship, I would probably be selling potatoes on the Waimanu Road." This received much applause and laughter from the audience.

The Indian community organisations in Fiji play a very active role in the socio-economic development of the community. Organisations like Shri Sanatan Dharam Sabha of Fiji, Arya Pratinidhi Sabha of Fiji, The India Sanmarga Ikya Sangam (TISI Sangam) not only look after the religious needs of the community but have been pioneers in setting up schools at a time when the colonial administration discouraged schooling for Indian children. The Sangam is the largest organisation of people of south Indian origin, running more than a dozen schools and a nursing college at Labasa besides a technical college.

People from South India were late comers in Fiji as migration from Madras port began only in 1906, nearly 30 years after Calcutta, and it came to a halt when the "girmitiya" system was abolished in 1920. Though these migrants came from what is now Tamil Nadu, Telangana and Kerala, their identity went through an interesting transition in the melting pot of Fiji. Grossly outnumbered among the "girmitiyas" in Fiji from the north, the migrants from the south adopted the already established Hindi-Awadhi-Bhojpuri mixed Fiji Baat as their language. And they also submerged their language ancestry to all become members of the Tamil Sangam, which became the language of all Indian people irrespective of the region they migrated from.

The Tamil Sangam also manages the old Siva Swami Subramanian Temple in Nadi. This is the most revered temple of the Tamil community in Fiji. When the temple had celebrated its silver anniversary in 1976, my father had laid the foundation stone for a new temple at the same premises.

The temple was to hold the Maha Kumbhabhishekam in 2006 which takes place once every 12th year.

The Sangam's president, Dorsami Naidu, asked for assistance to invite a great scholar from south India and a cultural group for the event. We arranged the visit of eminent educationist Prof. A. Gnanam who had been Vice Chancellor of four universities and Chairman of the Indian National Science Academy. Keeping in mind the sanctity of the occasion, we presented a copy of the epic book *Thirukkura*l which comprises the teachings of Saint Thiruvalluvar, to the Nadi temple. Prof. Gnanam visited Labasa town where the Sangam has an engineering and nursing college. Prof. Gnanam was able to advise the Sangam on possible collaborations and assistance from institutions in India.

Diplomatic life is not just a string of parties and receptions; in Fiji the Indian High Commissioner remains in great demand as a chief guest at a variety of events. I have been a politician, a member of Parliament and a minister but I discovered my oratorical skills in Fiji and I came to enjoy giving speeches.

All the Indian organisations hold their annual conventions in different towns. The 47th Annual Convention of the Sri Sanatan Dharam Sabha took place at Prince Charles Park, Nadi, on 13 April 2006. I was the Chief Guest and addressed a gathering of over 10,000 people. I commended the hard work done by these organisations to keep their culture, language and traditions alive.

Besides these organisations, there were several farmers' carnivals in different towns and the presence of the Indian High commissioner or any of his representatives was very much sought after. I sometimes sent my colleagues to represent the mission. Consular Officer Arun Sarkar went to attend the Labasa Sangam program and was delighted with the experience.

One of my officers repeatedly complained to me that he was always kept busy in the office so he was not able to go out on tour. A farmer's Carnival was forthcoming at Ba town and they had invited me, but I suggested my deputy's name. He was quite excited and put his staff on duty to collect material for his speech.

My speeches were always extempore and I was not comfortable with the papers or talking points prepared by the office. My deputy, on the other hand, was armed with a 20-page well researched paper on the history of "girmits".

Next day, he delivered his much worked-on speech before an audience of around 8,000 people. The program was to include cultural items, fashion parades and many more entertaining items. The Chief Guest was reading his speech, trying to enlighten the crowd about how their forefathers worked on the plantations in difficult conditions and how their hard work helped the coming generations to progress and prosper. But even before he had gone through half his speech, the crowd got restless and so he had to stop mid-way. He even forgot to declare the event open.

On his return, he looked very annoyed that his hard work done on preparing the speech had not been appreciated. He complained that I always began my speeches with a reference to "girmit" and ended with "girmit" but his audience was not willing to listen to a much more researched account with facts and figures. I jocularly told him that Fiji people listen to me because I have "girmit" blood in my veins to pacify him.

I mention this to make a point that there is a need to change our perceptions with the passage of time. The third fourth generation descendants of "girmitiyas" are now well-off farmers, businessmen, politicians, professionals doing well in all areas. They are not interested in listening to stories of the indignities faced by their ancestors. Also, the festivities are the main attraction. I gently explained to my younger colleague that one has to assess the audience's interest while speaking.

Besides the Hindu and Sikh organisations there are also the Fiji Muslim League, the Maunatul Islam of Fiji in Lautoka and the Ahmadiyya Muslim Jamat in Suva. One day, Justice Nazhat Shameem of the Fiji Supreme Court conveyed to Shiromani that the Ahmediyya Muslim Jamat would like to invite the Indian High Commissioner to their Salana Jalsa. The Ahmediyya global religious leader Mirza Masroor Ahmed was to be the chief guest and it would be inaugurated by Vice President Ratu Joni Madraiwiwi.

They were not sure of the protocol, but Shiro said that she did not see any reason why I should not accept their invitation. Shiro and I attended their annual convention on 27 April together with their leader, Mirza Masroor Ahmed and Vice-President, Ratu Joni.

I have always been a history buff and I gave an extempore speech on perceptions of Islam in changing times and Islamic history. My speech came as a surprise to many in the audience. Several Ahmediyya friends congratulated me later, saying that they had learnt many aspects of Islamic history that they had not known before. Ratu Joni jokingly said that I had a rapt audience. The next year I was invited as the Chief Guest to the Maunatul Islam's mosque to address the gathering at the Prophet Mohammad birth anniversary celebration.

Prime Minister Qarase's visit to India had turned the focus on Fiji and we had a number of visitors from India in Suva. The ICCR sent a renowned Bharatanatyam dancer, Yamini Muthanna, from Karnataka. Another eminent Veena player, Saraswathi Rajagopalan, also visited Fiji with her five-member team. Both artists performed at the Suva Civic centre on 8th July 2006. The programme was inaugurated by Vice-President Ratu Joni in the presence of former Prime Minister Mahendra Chaudhary and Mrs. Veermati Chaudhary.

Two ministerial visits took place in October 2006. Minister for Overseas Indian Affairs Vayalar Ravi visited Fiji on 18th October and inaugurated a Roundtable at University of Fiji on the situation of Indian Diaspora in Fiji. Less than a fortnight later, Minister of State, External Affairs, E. Ahamad visited Fiji for the Pacific Forum Dialogue Partners meeting at Nadi from 25th to 27thOctober 2006.

A Development cooperation agreement was signed for cooperation between the two countries in the fields of health, tourism, agriculture, civil aviation, water resources, sustainable development, information technology and other areas.

Vayalar Ravi was accorded a traditional Fijian welcome at the historic Biesese village, which was one of the first Indian settlements and also happened to be the native village of High Chief Ratu Josefa Ilioilo or Ratu Josefa Iloilovatu Uluivuda to give his full name, the third and then President of Fiji.

Indigenous Fijian life is based on the community and the village functions as a unit headed by the chief. Fijian ceremonies are elaborate affairs, stretching for a couple of hours with speeches, dances and presentation of gifts of food. The main part of the welcoming ceremony is based on the preparation and consumption of yaqona or kava, a mildly soporific drink.

(WebMD describes kava thus: Kava is a beverage or extract that is made from Piper methysticum, a plant native to the western Pacific islands. The name "kava" comes from the Polynesian word "awa," which means bitter. In the South Pacific, kava is a popular social drink. It is consumed as a beverage in ceremonies to promote relaxation.)

The preparation of kava is a highly ritualised solemn ceremony when an important guest is to be welcomed. The chief and the guests are seated on pandanus mats or, as a concession to western ways, on low chairs. The chief guest is presented with a tabua (a whale's tooth) and a Fijian man, acting as the guest's herald expresses thanks for the gift. Other gifts such as kava root, mats and bark cloth are presented in the same elaborately ritualised manner.

The kava ceremony then begins with the pounding of the root in a large wooden bowl amidst chanting by Fijian men, all bare chested and gleaming with a coating of coconut oil and wearing bark cloth and grass skirts. In ancient days, it is said the kava root was chewed to paste by young virgins!

The mashed kava is then mixed with water and strained. One of the men fills a small bowl, called bilo, made of coconut shell, with the brownish liquid and with great solemnity walks up on bended knees holding the bilo with outstretched arms, kneels down in front of the guest and offers him the bilo of yaqona. The bilo is accepted with three claps and drunk in a single draught.

I had explained the intricacies of the ceremony to the Minister in advance. I also warned him of the unfamiliar metallic taste of kava as unsuspecting guests have grimaced at tasting the kava.

Once the bilo is empty, everyone gives three rhythmic claps to the cry of matha that means it is finished. Kava is then served to the guest's herald and then to other guests and chiefs according to seniority. Kava drinking continues as the village girls dressed in bark cloth performing welcoming dances.

Vayalar Ravi was delighted by the traditional welcome conducted on the village green ringed with coconut palms with the sounds of the ocean in the distance in a setting so similar to his own state of Kerala.

The highlight of the visits that year was the arrival of the Indian naval ship, INS Tabar at Suva on a goodwill mission. INS Tabar was a new top-of-the-line stealth frigate of the Talwar class, commissioned two years ago in 2004.

It docked at Fiji's Suva Harbour for three days from 13th July 2006 and the day of its departure it held joint exercises with the Fiji Navy. There was a round of ceremonies and celebrations which were attended by the

Captain and senior officers of the ship. Indians in Fiji take great pride in the display of Indian capabilities. They attended the public functions in large numbers.

I hosted a dinner at India House for the officers of INS Tabar and invited all serving officers and former officers of the Fiji Military Forces. It was a grand affair. The warship had brought with them a ceremonial band which gave a performance on the lawns of the India House. They played a mix of Hindi Bollywood songs and old western favourites and concluded with the Indian and Fiji national anthems.

I had learned from my soldier father the tradition that when the regimental band was invited to play at a family function, the host ceremoniously presented a gift in appreciation to the band leader. Having watched my father do that on a couple of occasions I arranged for a crate of the best Jamaican rum.

When the band ended their performance, I turned to Col. Paul Manueli, whom I had seated next to me. He was a little startled when I asked him to do the honours. So, we walked over to the band, greeted them and Col. Manueli handed over the carton of rum to the band leader.

Paul Manueli was a highly decorated military officer and the first indigenous Commander of the Royal Fiji Military Forces. A graduate from Sandhurst, he was the chief architect of the Fiji Naval Service and the one who made possible Ratu Mara's dream of Fiji's participation with the Peace Keeping Forces of the United Nations. All subsequent commanders of the Fiji military, including the present prime minister Frank Bainimarama and his ministerial colleagues, Ratu Epeli Nailatikau and Ratu Epelu Ganilau and even the first coup perpetrator and former prime minister Sitiveni Rabuka had trained under Commander Paul Manueli. After retirement he became a successful businessman and also served as a cabinet minister.

As we were walking back Col. Manueli suddenly turned emotional; holding my hand he said, "Son, you have done me a great honour today." I was touched and replied, "Nothing less than that you deserve, Sir." He smiled and returned to his seat and the party went on.

My story of Fiji cannot be complete without the mention of Sir Moti Tikaram, widely hailed as "one of the greatest sons of Fiji" because of his many accomplishments. Son of "girmit" parents, who came to Fiji from a village in Uttar Pradesh's Firozabad district in 1912, he was the first local person to be appointed a Magistrate. Later he became the first Ombudsman of Fiji and also served as President of the Fiji Court of Appeals.

Sport was a passion for him. Fiji's main sport, as the world knows, is rugby but that game is played only by ethnic Fijians. In 1959 he took over as president of what was known as the 'Fiji Indian Football Association'. In the years and decades to come, it was his vision and drive that made soccer a truly national and multi-ethnic sport in Fiji.

Today, each province has its own team and club matches are keenly contested, drawing huge enthusiastic crowds. The Indian national team came on a tour of Fiji and I watched, with some chagrin, our team being trounced not only by the Fiji national team but also by one of the better provincial teams.

He had been a close friend of my father's and had also known my grandfather. I often turned to him for advice and guidance on indigenous Fijian customs and traditions. For me he was Uncle Moti. He was knighted in 1980 — one of only three Fiji-born Indians so honoured, apart from Sir Vijay Raghubir Singh, former Attorney-General, and Sir Sathi Narain, businessman and shipowner. But of all the awards and tokens of recognition he received, the one that was perhaps closest to his heart was the "Pravasi Bhartiya Samman" awarded to him by the Indian government in New Delhi in 2007. The two other Fiji nationals recipients of the award prior to him are former Prime Minister Mahendra Chaudhary and Golfer Vijay Singh and in 2010 Y P Reddy a prominent businessman and Chairman of the Fiji Girmit Council was awarded the same for community service.

For my wife and me it was our good fortune to have been able to spend time with him in August 2011 when we were visiting Fiji for a lecture I was invited to give on "India-China Relations" at the University of the South Pacific. He invited us to a lunch he was hosting for Sir Edmund Hillary's widow who was visiting Fiji. Our last memories will be of the quintessential Uncle Moti, the gracious host, exuding his old-style charm and dignity. He died on May 17, 2012 at Suva at the age of 87.

Even as we were busy with visitors from India and other activities, I felt a growing sense of unease over the Fijian political scene. The Fiji army chief, Commander Bainimarama continued to be bitterly opposed to the grant of amnesty to the leaders of the 2000 coup. Tensions had started brewing between the government and Commander Bainimarama which erupted in a public spat after the government released two plotters of the 2000 coup from prison.

Bainimarama also accused the Qarase government of corruption and racist policies. Dark rumours of a possible coup spread through Suva as the tussle between the Prime Minister and the Military commander played out for several months.

It was in this stormy atmosphere that the general elections were held in the month of May 2006. There were fears of political instability in case there was no clear verdict. Bainimarama had threatened to take action against Qarase for telling voters that there would be instability in the country if a non-Fijian was elected Prime Minister. The tension eased after Qarase formed the new government.

The new government's plans to introduce the Qoliqoli bill riled the military commander again. The bill proposed to transfer proprietary rights of qoliqoli areas (beach, lagoon and reef) from the State of Fiji to the qoliqoli owners, who are Fijians. The bill was criticised by the tourism industry and several parties as it would transfer all rights to the seabed, sand, reef, rivers and streams to private landowners. The war of words escalated as Qarase made an attempt to get President Iloilo to sack the military chief.

I watched the situation, growing convinced that Fiji was heading for a disaster, especially after the Police Commissioner, Andrew Hughes, an Australian national, sought to call in the military chief for questioning about deaths of some soldiers during the mutiny in 2000.

In this background the spokesperson of the Fiji Military accused the government of having lost its credibility. The military made nine demands of the government. Bainimarama gave a three-week ultimatum to the government to meet the demands or resign. A month later, Qarase visited Australia and was reported to have sought military assistance from the Australian government, which it declined.

Bainimarama also made a private visit to Australia and New Zealand at the same time. The media speculated that Qarase and Bainimarama had a secret meeting in Australia to try and reach a resolution to the differences between them. Qarase returned to Suva on 30th November and partially conceded to some of the demands. He agreed to suspend three bills and drop them altogether if a review found them unconstitutional. He also agreed to remove Police Commissioner Hughes. But the concessions were too little and too late for Bainimarama

Bianimarama rejected the offer and reiterated his ultimatum that Qarase accept all demands by noon of December 1st. He then extended the deadline to December 3 as the annual Rugby match between the Police and Military was to be held on December 2nd. The rugby match took place and the entire nation watched the exciting match in a relaxed and festive atmosphere. The military team defeated the police team.

This was in a way the trailer of forthcoming events. Taking advantage of this lull, the Qarase government moved to a secret location. On 3rd December Bainimarama announced that he had taken control of Fiji but Qarase emerged from hiding and claimed that he was still in charge.

The coup-in-waiting reached its climax the next day as Fiji slid into its fourth coup. Soldiers arrived at the Prime Minister's residence and took away his car keys as armed troops encircled the building, cutting off access to it. Fijian troops reached the Armed Police division headquarters at Nasinu and removed the weapons from the Armoury without any resistance from the police.

Qarase, who had moved out of his house to a secret location, tried to call a cabinet meeting but it was too late. The police were effectively disarmed as soldiers had set up roadblocks and the Cabinet could not hold its meeting.

Bainimarama then called a televised press conference and declared: "The military has taken over the government, has executive authority and the running of this country." He urged all citizens to remain calm. Eventually, President Illioillio dismissed the Parliament and thus Bainimarama took over control.

The coup of 2006 was a creeping coup where most of the moves were played out in public. Unlike previous coups, it was not accompanied with violence or rioting. It was a coup for which dates were pre-decided. Every day's events were known in advance like a play in which the *bidushak* (clown) appears and tells the audience what is to unfold before them.

There was great excitement within the diplomatic corps in Suva, with Ambassadors and High Commissioners consulting each other on likely developments. As Bainimarama took over, Australia, New Zealand, USA and the UK condemned the coup in harsh terms. They also imposed sanctions against Fiji, including restrictions on travel by senior members of the military and the Bainimarama regime and their families. This hit the Fijians hard as many of them had children studying in these countries or close relatives living there. Bainimarama brushed aside the western condemnation and moved towards greater interactions with China.

India was in a delicate position, having spent the previous year promoting India-Fiji relations with the Qarase government including a high profile visit by Qarase to India. India had reacted with strong condemnation to Fiji's earlier coups. Its reaction to Bainimarama's takeover was more restrained but it supported the move to again suspend Fiji from the Commonwealth.

The Indian government decision was to maintain distance from the military regime, but continue minimal official contact as it was not in India's interest to sever its ties with Fiji. The long period when diplomatic ties were cut after the first coup had been damaging to India's interests as well as the interests of Indians of Fiji. India's contacts with the Fiji Indians had been cut off, Indian scholarships and other assistance were disrupted and even the influx of young Fijians to study in India was impeded.

India had now many more bonds of cooperation with Fiji and the rest of the Pacific since that time. The Indian government had invested heavily in goodwill and cooperation with Fiji and the people of Fiji, not a single individual or government. The Mission adopted a low-profile policy in the weeks after the coup though we maintained discreet contact with government officials.

Unlike in 1987 and 2000, when the underlying cause of the coups was to take back power from what was perceived as Indian dominated governments, in 2006 it was due to differences between the army commander and the Prime Minister. The overthrow of the Bavadra and the Mahendra Chaudhry government was aimed at dislodging governments with a large Indian presence. But Bainimarama's bloodless coup did not target Indians but was a fight between two streams of Fijian thought. Indians were also critical of Qarase's bills granting amnesty and changing the land lease system, which while reforming the leasing system would also mean steep increase in land rentals.

The Indian community was not inimical to Bainimarama as he spoke about equity among the races and removing the distinctions between the Indian and ethnic Fijian communities, and placing all Fiji nationals on the same plane. He also sidelined the highly influential Fijian traditional elite, the Great Council of Chiefs, which had huge influence on Fijian politics including in selecting the President.

Yet, there were many influential "Indian" voices critical of our hands-off stance. Prof. Brij Lal, in a letter to the ministry of external affairs, expressed dismay about the soft and muted approach adopted by the government of India on the 2006 coup as against the hard position adopted by Australia, New Zealand, USA and European Union etc. In his opinion the military coup could not be treated as an internal matter of a country by a democratic country (like India). The military regime had abrogated the 1997 constitution, which had been internationally acclaimed multiracial equitable constitution. (The 1997 Constitution had been drafted by a three-member commission which had included Prof. Brij Lal.)

Prof. Brij Lal was not alone in expressing his opposition to the interim government's moves. Others who were also critical were mostly academics, who included Biman Prasad, Brij Lal, his wife Padma and her brother Wadan Narsey, all close to both me and Shiromani, and more so to Shiromani as Padma and Wadan knew her from their early years in the Toorak locality close to Shiromani's paternal family home.

Sometime in December Mahendra Chaudhary came to meet me. He was expecting a larger political role for himself in the coming days. He was particularly concerned about the continuation of Indian developmental assistance to Fiji, especially for the sugar industry. He also expressed concern about the closure of the Emperor Gold mine which left about 1700 without jobs including 500 in his Ba constituency and inquired about Indian assistance to revive the mining sector. I responded by strongly emphasising the need for an early return to democracy in Fiji. A few days after our conversation, Chaudhary joined Bainimarama's cabinet as Minister for Finance, National Planning, Public Enterprises and Sugar Industry.

In early February 2007 as the political situation settled down, I invited the Commander and all his Cabinet members to India House for dinner. This raised many eyebrows amongst the diplomatic community in Suva. The idea was to break the diplomatic ice with the new leaders.

My tenure as High Commissioner was to end in March 2007, but the External Affairs Ministry asked me to stay on in Suva for an additional three months because of the unstable political situation in Fiji.

Since my scheduled departure date was well known, I was already attending farewell functions, some of them quite emotional events. Organisations like Arya Pratinidhi Sabha, Stree Sewa Sabha, Poor Relief Society, Hindi Teachers' Association, Girmit Council, University of Fiji, Fiji Muslim League, Ahmadiya Jamaat, and others held farewell functions which were attended by members of both the previous government and the present regime. Shiromani and I left Fiji after a whirl of farewell functions on 7th June.

I was pleasantly surprised when shortly before I left Suva, Commander Bainimarama invited me for a farewell tea at the Queen Elizabeth Barracks military mess with all his senior officers in attendance. I had visited the army mess several times with my father. He was a frequent guest, invited by the group of old World War II veterans. I had personally never been invited to the army mess during my tenure, and that had rankled even though the times were very different.

It was a significant occasion and I was accompanied by my officers, Anil Anand and Prof. Mahavir Singh. Bainimarama, who still retained the position of Military commander, appreciated India's stance at the recent political happenings and commended my understanding of Fiji.

While Prof. Singh was explaining the activities of the Cultural Centre, he mentioned the yoga programmes being conducted at the Lautoka sub-centre. Commander Bainimarama asked whether the yoga teacher can be called at Suva for a few days to which I immediately responded certainly yes. He then snapped his fingers at his staff officer Col. Qiliho to get in touch with Professor Mahavir Singh to arrange a week-long programme for army officers by Yoga Teacher Chintapalli who was popularly known as Yogapalli in Fiji.

In another unusual gesture a farewell lunch was hosted by the government where all Cabinet ministers were present.

Subsequently, Commander Bainimarama organised a farewell dinner in my honour at the Officers Mess. Col. Paul Manueli was sitting next to the Commander. Yours truly and the third member of his beer swilling gang, Ratu Sir Edward Cakobau's son Ratu Epeli Nailatikau sat next to me.

Colonel Manueli began his toast with the words: "High Commissioner, you have followed in your illustrious father's footsteps in doing a very good job in bringing our two countries and our peoples close together. He would have been proud of you. I congratulate you on a good job done."

I replied: "Sir you are being kind to me. He was a colossus and I am a pygmy in front of him." He cut me off by saying, "High Commissioner you belittle yourself too much. I know he would have been proud of you just as I am."

My eyes moistened and it took me a few moments to regain my composure. Of all the praise and kind comments I have received for my work in Fiji, these words moved me the most; words that I deeply cherish and will always remember.

Shiromani later told me she was worried for a moment that I might lose my composure and embarrass myself. Having regained control I thanked Col. Manueli profusely and then tried to introduce some levity into the emotionally charged evening.

I was presented with a pair of long Fijian war clubs; highly polished wooden clubs which were the main weapon used by the warring tribes in olden times. Each club carried a silver plaque with my name and that of the RFMF (Republic of Fiji Military Forces). A high honour indeed!

They now have pride of place at the entrance to my study in my home in Gurgaon together with the tabua presented to my father by the Great Council of Chiefs of Fiji. The tabua has great significance in Fijian society and is the most precious gift to honour a person in recognition of his contribution to that society.

The two gifts marked the end of our tenures as Indian High Commissioner to Fiji but not the end of the Fiji love story which continues forever more.

VII
CHAPTER

Ni Sa Moce Fiji (Goodbye Fiji)

Mahavir Singh

Once it was known that Ajay Singh was finally leaving Fiji, farewell invitations from friends and various organisations and messages from friends and well wishers started pouring in. I cannot claim that I was privy to all the farewells, public and personal, especially the latter as his circle of friends and well wishers was large and cut cross party and community lines. However, some events were attended by me and for others mentioned here some printed material is available. Yet, some significant events may be missing from this mention.

The dominant reaction at the news of his leaving was dismay as it was widely felt that his tenure had been too short. Prof. Satendra Nandan, former minister in Mahendra Chaudhary's ministry and a prominent litterateur of Fiji, wrote in an email, "I feel sad you are leaving before we could talk more." Rajendra Prasad, author of *Tears in Paradise*, echoed him, "I thought that you would stay for some time to impart your mature wisdom to our leaders on how to tread along with care, caution and understanding. *Kal aaye the, aaj jaa rahe hein*!" (came yesterday and leaving today.)

What was truly striking was how in some of his farewell parties he made very candid comments about Fiji and yet how his observations were appreciated by enlightened Fijians. Speaking at a book release function at the university of Fiji on 15th May 2007, Ajay Singh recited his nazm of Muzaffar Razmi: *Ye Jabr bhi dekha hai, Tareekh ki nazron ne/Lamhon ne khata ki thi, sadiyon ne sazaa paayi,* in a not so oblique reference to Fiji's many coups. Reporting on the event, the *Fiji Times* quoted him as saying: "Fiji is still paying for the mistakes committed during the coup in 1987. The people will continue to pay for it for centuries to come until they realise what was right and what was wrong."

While speaking during the launch of Professor Satendra Nandan's book *The Loneliness of Islands* on 15th May, he said, "It only took a few seconds for the coup to happen and it would take centuries for the people to pay for it. The people will be punished for that." He said each of Fiji's three coups had taken the country backwards. "Before the 1987 coup, Fiji's economy was rising and the country was high up there. All that had been shattered. But I have total faith in the people of Fiji," he said. "After every disaster the people will try to bounce back through their own efforts."

In a subsequent email to Ajay Singh, Prof. Satendra Nandan wrote "Just a note to say how much I appreciated your close up conversation the other day. I was both moved and felt proud. Thank you for saying what needed to be articulated by so many of us - you did it with deep dignity, profound thought and genuine love for these our islands and India's embracing love and care. No one should ever have to apologise for that. Thank you."

Ajay Singh was felicitated in a big gathering at a farewell dinner organized by the Suva Indian community at the DAV Girls college in Samabula. Under the caption 'Indian Envoy to Return Home' *The Fiji Sun,* on Saturday, May 19, 2007 wrote: "Indian HC Ajay Singh has completed his 2 years term and will return home next month. Mr. Singh who has family ties with Fiji said, 'when he heard the news of his being posted in Fiji, he was glad because he knew that he was returning back to his roots'. During his two years in Fiji Mr. Singh has strengthened ties between India and Fiji."

In his remarks at the farewell by the Arya Pratinidhi Sabha of Fiji, its president, Kamlesh Arya, made it a point to highlight the fact that during the last coup, Mr. Singh had kept his counsel, unlike the missions of the USA, Australia and New Zealand had made critical statements. "Mr. Singh was the only republic's representative who had Fiji at heart and did not make statements on the issue," Mr. Arya noted in the presence of Justice Devendra Pathick, Gujarat Samaj President Babu Bhai Patel, Pandit Bhuvan Dutt and a host of other prominent Fiji citizens.

The farewell programme at University of Fiji was much more elaborate and in which several people from the western part ofViti Levu participated representing educational institutions, cultural and social organisations. Here Prof. Filipe Bole conducted the traditional Fijian farewell ceremony and presented a Tabua (whale's tooth considered a high honour) to Ajay Singh and read out his farewell address in Fijian language. Later, he sent me the English version of his speech.

In his speech he said: "With this *kamunaga* (whale's tooth) we wish to confirm and convey to you our deep respect and admiration for the outstanding achievements of your tenure as India's High Commissioner in Fiji. We believe that this has been due in no small measure to the deep rooted and wide and familiar connections that you have with Fiji and its people. Much of it too depends, no doubt on the wise and farsighted foreign policy of your government with respect to Fiji. We crave yours and your government's indulgence to continue to strengthen the ties between our two countries that you have so assiduously built and maintained during your term as India's High Commissioner in Fiji."

Prof. Bole before joining the University of Fiji had been an active politician in Fiji. He had served as a Cabinet Minister for Education, Fiji's Ambassador to the United States and the United Nations, Foreign Minister and the Deputy Prime Minister of Fiji at different intervals. He is known for his moderate views in politics.

After this ceremony, half a dozen speakers spoke and appreciated Ajay Singh's good work. Vice-Chancellor Professor Rajesh Chandra in his formal farewell address, said: "There is no doubt that he has been an outstanding success as India's HC to Fiji. He has helped Fiji get a better understanding of the new India and the many opportunities they hold for even closer and more fruitful relationship between Fiji and India. The visit of the former PM Qarase to India in 2005 provided fiji with a much greater appreciation not only of the high regards that india held Fiji in — the 70 member of the Fiji delegation on a state visit was given a red carpet treatment — but also of india's willingness to assist Fiji in a wide range of areas.

All through this crisis Shri Singh has managed a *blend of quiet diplomacy* designed to get Fiji on track for parliamentary elections and sustainable governance and development. India's constructive and thoughtful involvement with Fiji, I feel is being appreciated both here and in the Commonwealth. This comes from India's deep historical, cultural and diplomatic connections with and care for Fiji.

There is no doubt that the relationship between Fiji and India is poised for a significant expansion for mutual benefits and Shri Ajay Singh can take considerable credit for this. I hope I can be forgiven for suggesting that one such new horizon is The University of Fiji. At a personal level, I was fortunate that he was always generous with his time and advice.

He always reassured that the Fiji Uni was one of his top priorities. He also offered sound advice regarding the value of inclusion and working together with the government. I have no doubt that his good word put in with the government resulted in an improvement in the relationship between the government and the university.

In areas of cooperation in particular the Information and communication technology has a special place. We know that both for your father and for you better understanding between the Indigenous Fijians and Indo-Fijians was the highest priority. I think that you will see that in committing ourselves to the Centre for Indigenous Studies – and to the vision of a united Fiji based on better understanding among the two main ethnic groups we are honouring the efforts of both your father and yourself.

We also wish Shreemati Shiromani Singh well in future, Mrs. Singh has been much involved in the success of Shri Ajay Singh – we thank you Mrs. Singh very much for your own working Fiji both directly and in supporting his excellency.

Fiji is obviously very dear to both of you. We will miss both of you very much; pl keep in touch and look us when you return. Have a safe and enjoyable trip back to India. We wish both of you the best of health, happiness and success.

Vinaka Vakalevu, Dhanyawad, thank you."

The Hindi Teachers Association of Fiji at Suva, presented a plaque to Ajay Singh which stated:

> H E Mr. Ajay Singh, High Commissioner of India
>
> To Recognize the Assistance, Support And Guidance Provided to the Association During His Stay Here in Fiji

Manisha Ramrakha (President),

Vidya Singh (Treasurer), 30 May 2007.

Baleshwar Agrawal, founder Secretary General of the ARSP on learning that Ajay Singh was returning soon e-mailed him, "Your experience as Indian High Commissioner to Fiji will be useful to us when you come back to India."

June 6th was the last working day for Ajay Singh in Fiji. He went to the office as usual in the morning and after disposing of the necessary office work, handed over the charge to his deputy Anil Anand. He joined the staff over a cup of tea and left for India House for his onward journey to Nadi with Mrs. Shiromani Singh. I accompanied them to Nadi to see them off.

Mr. Madan Prasad, the official chauffeur of the Flag Car of the High Commissioner, drove us to Nadi. In the evening they met some friends in a cafe and for dinner with some friends in Denarau Island and spent the night in Raffles Hotel which is across the road from the Nadi Airport.

Next morning around six we left for the airport two hours prior to the departure of the flight. The Fiji government protocol officer facilitated their check in at the airport. As Madan Prasad and I waited at the airport for the flight to take off, Madan remarked in an emotional tone, "Sir, Ajay Singh *bahut badhia admi hain.*"

Ajay Singh had the ability to relate to people of all walks of life. While in Fiji, his great love for the islands was evident to all, and the people of Fiji responded to that sentiment in good measure.

Glossary

PRONOUNCIATION OF FIJIAN ALPHABETS

Fijian Spelling	*Phonetic Spelling*	*Fijian Spelling*	*Phonetic Spelling*
'B' as in 'Tabua'	MB (as in 'Number')	'G' as in 'Sigatoka'	NG (as in 'Sing)
'C' as in 'Cakobau'	TH (as in 'That')	'Q' as in 'Yaqona'	NGG (as in 'Finger')
'D' as in 'Nadi'	ND (as in 'End')		

FIJIAN WORDS, PRONOUNCIATION AND MEANINGS

Fijian Word	*Pronounced*	*Meaning*
Adi	Andi	Honorific for women of rank.
Bilo	Beelo	The half of a coconut shell by which'Yaqona' is served and drunk.
Mataqali	Matangali	Patrilineal descent-group.
Make	Maykay	Action-song; popular Fijian dance.
Ratu	Ratu	Native Fijian of noble Birth-a Chief (as opposed to common man).
Salu	Sooloo	Clothing, waist-cloth-almost like a Lungi in India.
Tabua	Tambua	Whale's tooth, used in ceremonies.
Tanoa	Tanoa	Bowl in which 'Yaqona'- the national drink of Fiji-is prepared.
Vunivalu	Vunivalu	Chiefly title.
Yaqona	Yanggona	National drink of Fijians; also known as 'Kawa' elsewhere in the Pacific Islands.

Sadhu- Mendicant
Melas- Village Fairs
Ratu- Chiefly Title
Kala Pani- Overseas Exile
Sardar- Headman
Pargana- Sub District
Thana- Police Station
Buggies- Horse Drawn Carriages
Jahaji- A fellow Traveller on a Ship
Bhikhari- Beggar
Kangal- Penniless
Aalah- A Folklore Song
Bhajans- Devotional Songs
Yaqona- Fiji's National Drink
Ikka- Carriage
Zanana- Ladies Section of the House
Majlis- Congregation
Tampatra- A Royal Order of Grant to a Temple etc.
Indenture System- A system of bonded labour instituted following the abolition of slavery by the British for crown colonies
Girmit- A term emerged as the distorted form of agreement
Coolie Lines- Dwelling Units of the Indenture workers on the plantations
Gaol- Prison
Arkatis- Recruiting Agents
Indo Fijian- Fiji Nationals of Indian descent
Faag- Songs of Holi festival

Photographs

Ajay Singh paying a courtesy visit to Tui Ba, Ratu Sairusi Nagagavoka. Seated in the middle is former secretary of the Girmit Council, Mr. Dwijendra Singh

Maneka Gandhi (in the centre) with Shiromani and Ajay Singh

Standing from left to right are Ajay Singh, S P Malviya, Kartar Singh, Chaudhary Charan Singh with stick in hand and Mulayam Singh Yadav at the other end

Ajay Singh with Former Prime Minister Chaudhary Charan Singh

Ajay Singh and Shiromani with Shri V P Singh and parents and family members of Shiromani Singh at Suva on the occasion of their wedding

Ajay Singh speaking on the occasion of the release of a postal stamp in the name of Chaudhary Charan Singh by government of India. Seated from left to right are: Mulayam Singh Yadav, Chaudhary Devi Lal, Shri Janeshwar Mishra, Chaudhary Ajit Singh, Vice-president of India Dr. Shankar Dayal Sharma, Janab Mohd. Yunus, Mrs. Gayatri Devi, H M Patel and Hemvati Nandan Bahuguna at the extreme end. Standing beside Ajay Singh is Jagdeep Dhankar.

Ajay Singh being administered oath of secrecy as a Minister by Shri R.Venkataraman, President of India at Rashtrpati Bhawan, New Delhi

Ajay Singh with Vice-President Ratu Joni Madraiwiwi after presenting his credentials as High Commissioner of India to Fiji at Suva. Shiromani Singh seated on the left of the Vice President and Sr. staff of VP office and IHC standing behind

Ajay Singh with George Fernandez in Dharamshala in Himachal Pradesh

Ajay Singh in conversation with K. Natwar Singh and Mrs. Natwar Singh

Ajay Singh with Aman Nath and Tony Bidesi at Neemrana Fort Palace office in Rajasthan

Standing from left to right Ajay Singh's father Captain Bhagwan Singh, Indian High Commissioner to Fiji, Mr. James Shankar Singh, Shiromani and Ajay Singh on the occasion of their engagement at India House, Suva. Standing next to Ajay Singh is Shiromani's father Pandit Sreedhar Maharaj

Ratu Sir Kamisese Mara first Prime Minister of Independent Fiji

Ajay Singh greeting His Holiness the Dalai Lama

Ajay Singh with Nelson Mandela at Taj Mahal in Agra

Ajay Singh with Sir Anand Satyanand and Lady Susan Satyanand on his right and Mr. Peter Adams and Mrs. Monika Adams on his left in Wellington

The marble Plaque at Devli building

Ajay Singh with Vijay Lakshmi Datt inaugurating the building constructed by Ajay Singh in memory of his wife Late Shiromani Singh at Devli village in Bharatpur, Rajasthan. Standing behind in turban is K. Darshan Singh and the village Sarpanch on the left of Vijay Lakshmi.

Minister for Overseas Indian Affairs Shri Vayalar Ravi inaugurated the Indian Culture Centre at the High Commission of India at Suva. Standing to his left are High Commissioner Ajay Singh and Joint Secretary, MOIA, Shri Malay Mishra and Prof. Mahavir Singh. On his right are Mrs. Shiromani Singh, Sir Moti Tika Ram and Mrs. Bhuvaneswari Singh

Babu Bere Singh and his friends from Fiji, Pandit Vishnu Deo on his left in the middle and J P Maharaj on his right. Jung Bahadur Singh is on the other end.

Ajay Singh and Shubha Singh with Father Captain Bhagwan Singh on their first arrival at Nausori Airport

Bharatnatyam Dancer Miss Yamini Muthanna being felicitated after a mesmerising performance at Suva Civic Centre. Standing on her right are Ratu Joni Madraiwiwi, Vice President of Fiji, Mrs. Shiromani Singh and Ajay Singh on extreme right. On the extreme left are Former Prime Minister Mahendra Chaudhary and Mrs. Veermati Chaudhary